PILGRIM
HEART

DARRYL TIPPENS

PILGRIM HEART

THE WAY OF JESUS
IN EVERYDAY LIFE

LEAFWOOD
PUBLISHERS

PILGRIM HEART
The Way of Jesus in Everyday Life
Published by Leafwood Publishers

Copyright 2006 by Darryl Tippens

ISBN 0-9767790-7-2
Printed in the United States of America

Walt McDonald, "With Mercy for All," *Blessings the Body Gave*

(Columbus: Ohio State University Press, 1998): 29. Reprinted by permission of the author.

Sections of Chapter 11 first appeared in "The Journey's the Thing: Reflections on Learning to Hear

God's Call," *Leaven* magazine 11.1 (2003): 29-33. Reprinted by permission of *Leaven* magazine.

Sections of Chapter 15 first appeared in "How Stories Save Us and Bring Us Home,"

New Wineskins (Sept. –Dec. 2003). www.wineskins.org

Reprinted by permission of *New Wineskins* magazine.

Scripture quotations, unless otherwise noted, are from the New Revised Standard Version of the

Bible. Copyright 1989 by the Division of Christian Education of the National Council of the

Churches of Christ in the USA. Used by permission.

Cover Design by Rick Gibson
Interior design by Greg Jackson, Thinkpen Design

For information contact:
Leafwood Publishers, Abilene, Texas
1-877-816-4455 toll free
www.leafwoodpublishers.com

06 07 08 09 10 11 12   13 14 / 10 9 8 7 6 5 4 3 2 1

To all those who have walked with me and shown me the way

". . . my fellow citizens and pilgrims,
some who have gone before,
some who follow after,
and some who are my companions in this life."

—AUGUSTINE,
CONFESSIONS (X.IV)

ACKNOWLEDGMENTS

This book is not only about life in a spiritual community. It is the product of life inside a vibrant fellowship of believers. I am deeply grateful to the many friends who patiently read drafts, made suggestions, and offered guidance along the way. Al Haley, my colleague and good friend, suggested many keen editorial improvements and countless insights into my subject—always with a measure of gracious encouragement. David Chatham, my former student, proved to be a prudent tutor as he read drafts and offered a number of helpful recommendations. I must also express particular thanks to Jennifer Adkison for her unfaltering research and proofreading skills.

I am immensely thankful to a regular gathering of rare friends who "tested" this work by reading the chapters and practicing the disciplines along with me over many months. These faithful companions include Leslie Alford, Roger Alford, Brad Livingstone, Linda Livingstone, Virginia Milstead, Zac Evans, Regan Schaffer, Robert Schaffer, Michael Williams, and Michelle Williams. Many others have offered helpful suggestions and solid encouragement along the way: Kyle Tippens, Jeff Tippens, Larry Kay, Aaron Kadoch, Lindy Adams, Ken Adams, Stacy Obenhaus, and Peter Cofield, among others. All these companions on the journey have taught me important lessons about an embodied spirituality.

When I consider the meaning of anamchara, *as discussed in Chapter 7, I am mindful of three particular soul-friends and faithful guides: Leonard Allen, my patient editor, insistent publisher, and wise friend, who nudged me towards the goal; Mike Cope, who has been the shepherd of my pilgrim heart for many years; and, above all, Anne, my all-time favorite editor, friend, and muse, who has provided a bounty of inspiration, gentle critique, and loving companionship for thirty-nine years.*

Darryl Tippens

PRAYER (I)

Prayer the Church's banquet, angels' age,
　　God's breath in man returning to his birth,
　　The soul in paraphrase, heart in pilgrimage.
The Christian plummet sounding heav'n and earth;
Engine against th' Almighty, sinners' tower,
　　Reversèd thunder, Christ-side-piercing spear,
　　The six-days' world transposing in an hour,
A kind of tune, which all things hear and fear;
Softness, and peace, and joy, and love, and bliss,
　　Exalted manna, gladness of the best,
　　Heaven in ordinary, man well dressed,
The milky way, the bird of Paradise,
　　Church-bells beyond the stars heard, the soul's blood,
　　The land of spices; something understood.

George Herbert
The Temple (1633)

TABLE OF CONTENTS

INTRODUCTION:
AN INVITATION TO BEGIN AGAIN

So dare to be as he once was, who came to live, and love, and die.
—Delores Dufner

The church exists for no other purpose but to draw men into Christ,
to make them little Christs.
—C. S. Lewis

We are living in an age of profound interest in spirituality. Movie stars, business executives, athletes, and intellectuals routinely pronounce themselves "spiritual." The menu of choices is wide and deep. Eastern, feminist, Native American, Jewish, Islamic, and Christian spiritualities beckon. The spirituality industry is booming, one database reporting more than 10,000 books on the subject. So one can fairly ask, why another one?

First, while there are many "spiritualities" abroad today, the subject of this book concerns a particular type. Writers who call for the kind of radical living as envisioned by Scripture and practiced by the saints[1] through the ages are not so numerous. Jesus invites us to journey on an arduous and narrow way that only a few are willing to risk: "For the gate is narrow and the road is hard that leads to life, and there are few that find it" (Matthew 7:14). Second, despite the wealth of books even on Christian spirituality, there are things yet to be said. Too many discussions of spirituality emphasize the private and interior dimensions, neglecting the richly *embodied* and *communal* nature of life in Christ. While acknowledging the interior dimensions to spiritual growth, this book celebrates *incarnational* practices that fully honor the social, practical, and embodied aspects of the way of Jesus.

Christianity is far more than a set of beliefs or a compelling intellectual vision; it is also a comprehensive way of life. Along with what Jesus and the disciples have taught us, we also must consider closely what they *practiced*—in their homes, on the road, in the marketplace. This book, therefore, is an invitation to consider afresh what it means to live like Jesus.

Although it may sound a bit strange to the ear, Jesus advocated a kind of "worldly" spirituality, that is, a way of life to be practiced daily. What would this in-the-world discipleship look like? A fair amount of clearing out and cleaning up must be undertaken before one can answer the question, for there is much that even Christians have gotten wrong about following Jesus. The original and pristine call of Jesus has been tainted, often subtly and invisibly, by systems of thought essentially alien to Jesus' world. Yet these philosophical systems have become so much a part of our way of thinking that their influences are mostly invisible to us. Add to these the numerous but faulty assumptions of popular culture about what it means to be "spiritual," and we have a good deal of confusion on our hands.

At the heart of Jesus' call is the urgency not just to believe what he taught, but *to act like him*. Being like Jesus is the alpha and the omega of the Christian life. Jesus said, "A disciple is not above the teacher, everyone who is fully qualified will be like the teacher" (Luke 6:40). John the Apostle urged Jesus' followers to love others to the degree and in the manner of Jesus himself: "As he is, so are we in this world" (1 John 4:17).

But how is it possible to be in the world as Jesus Christ is in the world? What would this mean for our lives and our churches? The New Testament presupposes that we are not only called to perform the deeds of Jesus, but we are empowered by his indwelling Spirit to *become* Jesus to the world. According to Paul, Christ dwells in every believer, shaping them and turning them into his *very likeness*.[2]

WITH FEET FIRMLY PLANTED

Sigmund Freud once accused Christians of trying to "fall off the earth," that is, to deny their essential humanity in their quest to be holy. His critique might apply to the religion of our day as much as to his own. Christians do not need to renounce the creation to be godly. On the contrary, they are called to enter deeply into the world. An incarnational spirituality *requires* them to consider how their bodies and their placement within vibrant communities are necessary aspects of their calling. They must discover and embrace the concrete practices that not only express their faith, but which nurture and form it. Far from "falling off the earth," followers should have their feet firmly planted in the earth. All of life is the proper arena for divine activity.

What is needed, then, is a God-focused spirituality that is also, paradoxically, creation-centered. C. S. Lewis expressed the point with characteristic conciseness:

> There is no good trying to be more spiritual than God. God never meant man [or woman] to be a purely spiritual creature. That is why He uses material things like bread and wine to put new life into us. We may think this rather crude and unspiritual. God does not: He invented eating. He likes matter. He invented it.[3]

Lewis is warning us against overly "spiritual" spiritualities, which enjoy a seductive appeal, but which also prove hollow and self-defeating. The way of Jesus not only takes account of the soul—it takes full account of the body and the created world in which our bodies are squarely placed.

A SPIRITUAL RENAISSANCE

Churches seem to be heading in quite different directions in our time, some flourishing, others wasting away. In the case of the latter, the quality of the teaching and the means of delivery may be more sophisticated and more "high tech" than ever, yet these churches may actually be less able to transmit the faith to their children than in the past. Given the considerable resources available today, how could this be? Part of the failure may derive from a naïve understanding of how faith is transmitted inter-generationally. In the quest to convey the right message, we may be abandoning the most basic—and most powerful—"tools" of faith transmission. Our ministers may be highly degreed, our staffs highly specialized, and our worship services elegantly orchestrated; but these are insufficient if we are not also actively engaging in the basic communal practices that are known to transmit spiritual memory and transform lives.

Just as whole societies in the West are losing their cultural memories, and just as some advanced societies are quite literally losing the will or the capacity to reproduce (note the dramatic decline in birth rates in "old" Europe and the simultaneous, deliberate denial of Europe's religious heritage), so also churches can lose the will, the knowledge, or the capacity to reproduce themselves. A community without the ability to regenerate is, by definition, "terminal." Charles Williams recognized the danger in the last century:

> There is not another institution which suffers from time so much as religion. At the moment when it is remotely possible that a whole generation might have learned something both of theory and practice, the learners and their learning are removed by death, and the church is confronted with the necessity of beginning all over again. The whole labour of regenerating mankind has to begin again every thirty years or so.[4]

The lesson is obvious. No matter how well we might have "done church" a generation ago, it matters little if we do not continually recreate the kind of compelling culture that allowed the early church to thrive in persecution and that will ensure the propagation of communities of faith in our time as well.

The failure to do this will be costly, indeed. While the gates of hell will not prevail against the kingdom of heaven, it is altogether possible that segments of the church of God will vanish from the earth in the next generation. Jesus once posed the most penetrating of questions: *"When the Son of Man comes again, will he find faith on the earth?"* (Luke 18:8). He did not answer his own question. I gather that he continues to place this query before us today. Two answers seem plausible: Either we choose spiritual malaise and inevitable extinction, or we choose the renewal that comes through radical discipleship.

Today many theologians and church leaders are calling us back to robust practices of the faith as expressed in early forms of Christianity.[5] A fresh look at Scripture and the experience of believers through the centuries teaches us to practice an embodied spirituality within living communities. Evidences of a spiritual renaissance are not hard to find. Throughout North America, in small towns and in large cities, we see promising signs of spiritual revival; and the evidences are even more pronounced in other quarters of the world, especially in developing nations and in the southern continents. We are on the threshold of a new era in the history of Christianity, when disciples from many different ethnicities and traditions are converging at a common point of understanding.[6] Despite their disparate origins and histories, believers seem to be arriving at a consensus that a full-bodied, Christ-centered spirituality is what we most need.

The growing emphasis upon an embodied spirituality should be good news since most of us make such poor angels anyway. It's a relief to learn that God expects us to be only human. However, be forewarned. The way of Jesus, practiced "on the ground" and in the body, is truly radical. Once we expose the Platonic and Cartesian threads within the fabric of our faith, once we remove the modernist contaminations of our practice, once we return to this earthy, biblical spirituality, we will find ourselves both liberated and disoriented. Our spirituality will almost surely look, feel, and wear differently. We will begin to think about ourselves as human beings in new ways; and, by extension, we will rethink our relationship to God and what it means to follow Jesus. The invitation to begin again is the hallmark of the Christian message: We are fallen; we are broken; yet we are loved, and Jesus continually invites us to begin...again.

PART ONE

INVITATION TO
THE JOURNEY

1

THE CALL TO A 'WORLDLY' SPIRITUALITY

Preach the gospel always. If necessary use words.
—Francis of Assisi

The discovery of God lies in the daily and the ordinary, not in
the spectacular and the heroic. If we cannot find God in the routines
of home and shop, then we will not find him at all.
—Richard Foster

Emily Dickinson, the brilliant belle of Amherst, has long intrigued me. A few years ago I made my pilgrimage to her home in Amherst, Massachusetts, hoping to capture something of the spirit of this ingenious poet who was "a great mystery and a constant surprise" to everyone, as her cousin once recalled. I stood in her upstairs, Victorian-era bedroom, looking out her window, remembering how she used to let baskets of cookies down on a rope to neighborhood children. Though she wouldn't talk to them directly, she would send them gifts from a distance. I looked across the street at the First Church of Amherst to which her family had belonged, but Emily had refused to attend.

Recalling her letters and poems, which are personal favorites, I have often wondered: Why did she find participation in community so difficult? Was there something wrong with the church across the street? Was her father too harsh, too puritanical and authoritarian? Was it the cold Calvinism preached from the pulpit that kept her away? Did the new science create too much intellectual doubt for her? Or was there something else inside young Emily that made connection with a community of faith impossible?

A partial explanation for Dickinson's "emotional seclusion" is the influence of Romanticism on her young mind, a philosophy which encouraged her to revere rebellion, solitariness, and separation from community.[1] One sees this theme in many of America's most influential thinkers—Thoreau and Emerson, for example—and it appealed to Dickinson. So, she could write, "A letter always seemed to me like Immortality, for is it not the *mind alone, without corporeal friend?*" (my emphasis).[2] She found "a spectral power in thought that walks alone."[3] In privileging mind and spirit over matter, in the denial of human company and even, to some degree, the physical world, Dickinson moved dangerously close to Gnosticism, an ancient philosophy that taught a distrust of the body and of material creation.[4]

At a young age, she entertained grave doubts about her material nature: "I do not care for the body. I love the timid soul, the blushing, shrinking soul...." she wrote to her cousin Abiah Root.[5] "[T]he mind alone without corporeal form" is what Dickinson honored most—a cerebral, interior, and disembodied spirituality.[6] The consequences of such a worldview are large—the dissolution of community, loneliness, and alienation. She is, in her own words, "homeless at home."[7]

I consider the plight of this remarkable American writer because she shows what can happen when spirituality is divorced from community. Dickinson is only an extreme version of the privatized spirituality that tempts many people today. The poet prophetically anticipated those who say, "I am spiritual, but not religious; I believe in the soul, but I don't need the church; I have a rich interior life, so what I do with my body doesn't matter." Dickinson, brilliant and beloved, is the prototype of the modern soul, hunched over the computer, dashing off messages to distant correspondents around the world ("This is my letter to the world / that never wrote to me," Dickinson writes plaintively), but sadly alienated from those in the next room or next door.

BETWEEN EMILY AND JESUS

If Dickinson's transcendental path represents one direction of a spiritual life, mine represents another. Yet the options that faced the poet are not too different from those that faced me as a young man—the lure of a cerebral, spiritualized world on the one hand; a concrete and embodied, and richly social one on the other. Like every follower of Jesus, I am the product of literal and spiritual forebears, in the flesh and in the faith. My town was home to several churches representing various streams of the Christian faith. My church, like a number of others, was birthed in the nineteenth century, when Enlightenment philosophies had had time to percolate into the popular consciousness.

In such an environment my theology of creation was a bit incoherent and undeveloped, while my understanding of sin, redemption, and eternal judgment was robust. This theological imbalance had an obvious effect on me. Popular notions that the body is inherently suspect competed with the Bible's claim that the body is the temple of God's Spirit. There was a marked emphasis upon the afterlife ("eternal salvation") and a general neglect of what is happening here and now. I heard a devotion to order and argument in nearly every sermon and Sunday school lesson, but a general distrust of mystery and emotion. One might judge such a religious life inadequate on several grounds, but in retrospect I am grateful for what I received. The gifts of this community included spiritual insight through immersion in Scripture; inspiration in the lives of those who modeled obedience; and a faithful way of life learned through a rich set of practices.

Miroslav Volf maintains that most people who come to faith do so because "they find themselves already engaged in Christian practices (say, by being raised in a Christian home) or because they are attracted to them. In most cases, Christian practices come first and Christian beliefs follow—or rather, beliefs are already entailed in practices...."[8] So it was with me. Stanley Hauerwas argues that much of the success of Catholicism derives from

> its ability to sustain Christianity as a way of life for peasants. To state the matter in this way will seem to many, both Catholic and Protestant, to put Catholicism in a negative light. Yet I mean such a characterization to be nothing but positive. First of all, I do not think there is anything wrong with being a "peasant," that is, someone who works every day at those

duties necessary for us to eat, to have shelter, to sustain the having of children and to carry on the basic practices necessary to sustain communities. Peasants may not be "intellectuals," but they have knowledge habituated in their bodies that must be passed on from one generation to another. Peasants are often suspicious of intellectuals because they rightly worry about "ideas" that come from people who do not work with their hands. Christian peasants usually do not think they are called to be holy. It is enough that they pray, obey, and pay....[O]ne of the great virtues of such a Christianity is its capacity to be practiced by people who are poor. Such a Christianity is not a set of beliefs or doctrines in order to be a Christian, but rather Christianity is to have one's body shaped, one's habits determined, in such a manner that the worship of God is unavoidable.[9]

My faith journey began in a community similar to the one described by Hauerwas. Spiritual formation consisted of an array of concrete practices, "low church" Protestant ones to be sure, but practices "habituated" in the body. I found faith in the sacraments of worship, particularly the weekly observance of communion, but also in frequent church meetings; Sunday school; vacation Bible school; monthly music services called "singings"; weekly youth meetings and regional youth rallies where I learned to speak in public; church camp; fellowship meals; and in revivals ("gospel meetings") that culminated in public confessions of sin, testimonies of faith in Christ, and baptisms.

In addition, there were various manifestations of religious practice in the life of the whole community. Christmas and Easter had not yet become wholly secular observances. Bibles were distributed to all elementary-age students by the Gideons; assemblies and sporting events opened with prayer; and communal prayer could be heard each noonday in the elementary school lunchroom. While I am not arguing for the appropriateness of such activities in today's multicultural society, I can say that these practices constituted a communal way of life for me as a young man. They made the worship of God "inevitable," in Hauerwas's terms.

My community, whatever its flaws, gave me the resources for growth. By the time I publicly acknowledged my faith in Christ at age fourteen, I had heard hundreds of sermons, had read much of the Bible, had attended countless revival meetings, and had memorized dozens, if not hundreds, of revival songs and hymns from my *a cappella* tradition. It is impossible to recall all the experiences that might have prompted me to enter the baptismal waters so many years ago, but I venture to say that it was the sheer kindness of Jesus' followers that had the greatest impact of all. In the preacher who baptized me, the women and men who taught me, the kindly neighbor who introduced me to missionaries, religious publications, and Christian colleges, I found encouragement and inspiration. I was the beneficiary of many spiritual gifts from these generous people. Though their theology may have been thin in places, they were Christ to me. Their love, expressed through prayer, singing, devotion to Scripture, and selfless service, continually beckoned to me.

As I grew I discovered the other side of the faith equation, the one characterized by transcendence and mystery. It is ironic that the final task of rationality was to announce its own limitations, to open the door to a way that goes deeper, more in tune with the ultimately ineffable nature of God. The head points the way to the heart.[10] I came to know *about* God through my early initiation; I have come to *know* God through a life of Christian practices, embodied in community.

FEASTING AND THE PILGRIM HEART

Like many today, Emily Dickinson tried to find her spirituality in isolation— separate from a community of believers and alienated from her own body. There was a time in my life when Dickinson's approach attracted me, but eventually I returned to Jesus' way, for it respects and honors our fully embodied nature. For Dickinson, "the supper of the heart" begins *after* the guest has departed, but I found such ethereal "meals" lonely, deficient, and—finally—spiritually dangerous. The true pilgrim heart needs flesh-and-blood companions and substantial food.

When Jesus presents spiritual health, he often does so in terms of lavish communal celebrations. He is the great wine-maker in John's gospel. Reunions, feasts, weddings, and banquets permeate the gospel accounts of Jesus' life, so much so that Jesus' critics accused him of being a kind of "party animal": "the Son of Man has come eating and drinking, and you say, 'Look, a glutton and a drunkard'..." (Luke 7:34). For two thousand years, a meal has served as the central event in weekly

Christian worship. Indeed, heaven will be the scene of a magnificent banquet of which all earthly feasts are but faint foreshadowings. Jesus' spirituality does not deny the material creation; rather, it revalues and transforms it.

Just as Jesus' spirituality involves feasting, it also involves traveling. True spirituality is never sedentary. Jesus was quite literally an itinerant teacher. Like other great "peripatetic" teachers of the ancient world, he taught as he walked. It's a general theme of the Bible that people of faith are travelers at heart: Abraham and Sarah, of course, but also Moses, the people of Israel, and the followers of Jesus. Moving towards God requires *pilgrimage*. When the first disciples met Jesus, they moved towards him; they went home with him; they abode with him (John 1:35-39). And while abiding with Jesus they *saw* as much as they heard. Jesus' wisdom was enfleshed in a variety of concrete activities (e.g., eating, touching, washing feet, healing, praying, reading Scripture, worshiping, etc.). In other words, he didn't merely teach the good news; he *performed* it. His wisdom was "caught" as much as it was "taught." In such a robust, multi-dimensional setting, "church" was hardly a formal institution. It was, instead, a distinctive *pattern of life*, a way of living in the world. It should not be surprising that the first name for Jesus' followers was "The Way."[11]

A follower of Jesus is a "pilgrim" (from the Latin *peregrinus*), literally one from a foreign land, an alien, a traveler. The faithful are "strangers and foreigners on the earth, [who]...are seeking a homeland...a better country, that is a heavenly one" (Hebrews 11:13-16). The language of pilgrimage permeates the literature of Christian spirituality. It is a central theme of Augustine's great autobiography, *Confessions*. It inspired the John Bunyan classic *Pilgrim's Progress*. It is a prominent figure of speech in Governor Bradford's 1630 exhortation to the faithful who sailed to New England (which is why every Thanksgiving we talk of "Pilgrims"). The metaphor of pilgrimage appears in the sermons of Cotton Mather, in the poetry of George Herbert, and in the venerable songs of the church, such as Samuel Stennett's eighteenth-century hymn:

> I am bound for the promised land,
> I am bound for the promised land;
> O who will come and go with me?
> I am bound for the promised land.

TRAVELING IN COMMUNITY

The song asks, "O who will come and go *with me?*" Following Jesus is not a solo enterprise. In the Middle Ages, the great era of pilgrimages to holy sites, pilgrims traveled in large groups for safety. Geoffrey Chaucer's pilgrims, for example, consisted of a group of thirty-one because the route from London to Canterbury passed through treacherous forests where robbers lay in wait. The Christian life is such a journey: a long, sometimes bumpy, circuitous, and risky adventure. Thus, when the Lord commissioned his twelve apostles, he sent them out two by two (Mark 6:7), as he sent out the seventy emissaries of the good news in pairs (Luke 10:1).

Wherever he goes, Jesus forms communities. Hence, one of the sayings of the Desert Fathers: "If you see a young man climbing up to heaven by his own will, seize him by the foot and pull him down, for this is to his own profit."[12] This odd bit of advice makes sense if one understands that spirituality is learned and confirmed in relationship. This is not unlike the African proverb: "If you want to go fast, go alone; but if you want to go far, go together." As we travel in each other's company, we not only find safety and encouragement, we find Jesus himself, walking beside us (Luke 24:13-35). From the beginning *Jesus meant for us to go together*, and *church* is a name for the group of people who follow Jesus together.

And what is it that we do "on the road"? The chapter that follows considers further the meaning of an embodied or incarnational spirituality, while Chapters 3 through 17 introduce specific, selected practices that encourage spiritual growth. The number of practices that might have been considered in a book like this is quite large, for disciples have engaged in literally dozens of spiritual exercises for the last two thousand years. The ones discussed here are in particular danger of being under-valued or neglected. Indeed, some of them, while generally admired, are considered "secular," and therefore ignored. Such a division into "sacred" and "secular" needs to be rethought. Perhaps the following discussion will stir all pilgrims to see with fresh eyes just how the life of Jesus can be "performed" in a great variety of ordinary routines in everyday life.

2

THE BLESSING OF
BODY AND SOUL

Or do you not know that your body is a temple of the
Holy Spirit within you, which you have from God?
...therefore, glorify God in your body.
1 Corinthians 7:19-20

Let us love the country of here below. It is real....
It is this country that God has given us to love.
—Simone Weil

In her beautiful, Pulitzer-Prize-winning novel, *Gilead*, Marilynne Robinson tells the story of an aging minister, John Ames, who writes a long letter to convey to his beloved son the sum of his wisdom, as the old minister faces death. In one particularly moving scene, Ames reminds his son of the day he gave him communion, after the Sunday service had concluded:

> [W]hen almost everyone had left and the elements were still on the table and the candles still burning, your mother brought you up the aisle to me and said, "You ought to give him some of that." You're too young, of course, but she was completely right. Body of Christ, broken for you. Blood of Christ, shed for you. Your solemn and beautiful child face lifted up to receive these mysteries at my hands. They are the most wonderful mystery, body and blood.

The minister explains to the boy what is on his mind:

> I have been thinking a great deal about the body these last weeks. Blessed
> and broken....I wanted to talk about the gift of physical particularity and
> how blessing and sacrament are mediated through it. I have been thinking
> lately how I have loved my physical life.[1]

The minister's attention to the body as blessed, broken, and particular is fundamentally Christian, yet it is little understood today.

Since life in the Spirit means going on a journey, it follows that it must occur in particular places on the map of this world; and it must occur through the medium of our bodies. Once one realizes that Christianity is a way of life and a journey, one must consider the importance of the body, for it is bodies that perform actions and go on journeys. This point should be obvious, yet it is so often overlooked, it merits our reflection.

Many Christians hold a view of the body that borders on heresy.[2] They have gotten their notions of the body from Plato and his followers, from Descartes, or from modern descendents of a certain form of Puritanism, the result being a suspicion of—or even a hatred of—the body. Scripture, however, teaches that the body is from the Lord and for the Lord. Genesis describes a God who is delighted with his creation of human beings out of the soil (Genesis 1-2). In the New Testament view, our bodies are temples of the Spirit and sacred offerings to God (1 Corinthians 3:16-17; Romans 12:1). Christian orthodoxy is rooted in the truth of the "incarnation"—that God became flesh. God chose to become a human being with a real body ("he was revealed in the flesh," 1 Timothy 3:16). The human body is so important to God that he plans to transform it and preserve it eternally (1 Corinthians 15:42-49). Given the sacredness of the body, followers of Jesus appreciate the body, not merely as a "vehicle" of good works or the temporary "container" of God's Spirit, but as something intrinsically and eternally valuable, something worthy of care, respect, and transformation.

Yet doubts about the body have nagged Christians for centuries, and the doubt continues today. I recall giving a lesson in a chapel service at a Christian university in which I emphasized the importance of the human body to God—as seen in God's intention to redeem the body and raise it up for eternal life in the resurrection

(Romans 8:23 and 1 Corinthians 15:12-57). After I spoke, an indignant student approached me with an objection. What I said about the eternal importance of bodies—redeemed bodies!—couldn't possibly be true, she complained, because she had grown up in the church, having never heard such a thing.

WHEN SPIRITUALITY IS "TOO SPIRITUAL"

My young critic belongs to a large company of those who are far more Platonic in their view of the body (the "soul" is eternal, the "body" temporary), than they are biblical. A pervasive Platonism (or Neoplatonism) has greatly affected the thought and language of Christians. So, Meister Eckhart, the German medieval mystic, implies the basic triviality of the body compared to the soul: "The shell must be cracked apart if what is in it is to come out, for if you want the kernel, you must break the shell."[3] In the analogy, the soul is the kernel, and the body is the mere container, something to be discarded once the valuable contents have been retrieved. With such a view, the trivialization or the denigration of the body is not far behind.

Stanley Hauerwas points out that the problem with today's spiritualities is that they are "too spiritual." A Cartesian mind-body dualism has misled us into believing that faithfulness is principally "right thinking" about God: "If we have any hope of reclaiming the church as a disciplined body of disciples...we need to recover the discipline of the body that at least offers an alternative to the endemic individualism and rationalism of modernity," says Hauerwas.[4] The Bible presents a spirituality that is not escapist; rather, it envisions a holy way of life that includes the eventual redemption of our bodies—holy, renewed, and transformed, yes—but bodies nonetheless. Paul imagines a spirituality in and through the body, not exclusive of it: "Present your bodies as a living sacrifice, which is your spiritual worship" (Romans 12:1).

Dietrich Bonhoeffer, imprisoned by the Nazis and separated from family, friends, and fiancée, was troubled by a form of spirituality that rejected the values of this life:

> I am sure we ought to love God in our *lives* and in all the blessings he sends us. We should trust him in our lives, so that when our time comes, but not

before, we may go to him in love and trust and joy. But, speaking frankly, to long for the transcendent when you are in your wife's arms, to put it mildly, a lack of taste, and it is certainly not what God expects of us. We ought to find God and love him in the blessings he sends us. If he pleases to grant us some overwhelming earthly bliss, we ought not to try and be more religious than God himself.[5]

As a condemned prisoner, Bonhoeffer well knew the transitory nature of earthly joys, but he also believed that the blessings of the body are divine gifts for which we should be thankful.

I dwell on this point because many today suffer from negative views of the body, which lead to serious eating disorders, forms of self-mutilation, and other destructive behaviors. I was for many years attracted to a version of disembodied spirituality, not unlike what tempted Emily Dickinson. I was drawn to intellectual abstraction, and I immersed myself in countless books on spirituality. I was misled by a confusing slippage in the use of terms, especially with regard to "flesh" and "spirit." "Flesh" in Paul's language does not usually mean the body, but rather the part of the self in rebellion against God. "Flesh" is more attitude and will than blood or muscle. For example, in his condemnation of the sins of the "flesh," Paul cites dispositions of the heart like anger, jealousy, and envy that can be practiced without the body's involvement at all. The body is, by contrast, part of the material order of creation, which God pronounces good. "The earth is the Lord's and the fullness thereof." It is something so sacred it can be both a temple worthy of God's habitation and a sacred sacrifice offered to God. As a youth growing up in the church, I did not learn these distinctions, and so I pursued an otherworldly, "spiritual" existence.

The intellectual life constituted another kind of temptation. Though it was largely unconscious, I decided that I would *think* my way into the presence of God. Surely, if I read the greatest writers and absorbed their thoughts, then I would find the key to life's problems. Since the intellectual life requires a kind of asceticism that is not unlike religious self-denial, all this seemed perfectly consistent. Yet I became discouraged along the way. Any asceticism—whether religious or intellectual—that leads one to deny his or her own embodied nature is finally going to fail. It didn't seem to work for Emily Dickinson, and it didn't work for me. It took me some time, after many disappointments, to discover that my own ascetic approach to the spiritual life was flawed, exactly as Paul had warned: "Such conduct may have an air of wisdom, with its forced piety, its self-mortification, and its severity to the body; but it is of no use at all in combating sensuality" (Colossians 2:23, Revised English Bible). Through the good counsel of wise friends and the discovery of an incarnational spirituality, I found a better way. It involves believing with our bodies, not against them.

THE BELIEVING BODY

A better theology and a better psychology show us how to believe with our minds, while at the same time *believing in and through our bodies*. This approach reflects how heart, mind, soul, and body are intimately and inevitably bound together in the worldviews of the biblical writers. Consider Abraham on the road to the Promised Land (Genesis 12:1). It's not necessarily the case that Abraham believed in his head, then put his body into gear, packing up, saying his good-byes in Ur, getting out the maps, and heading to the land of promise. This simple, sequential view of things (thought leading to action) does not quite match how human beings function. Abraham not only believed before he acted, *he believed in and through his actions*. Abraham believed before he became a pilgrim, no doubt, but his pilgrim heart became ever more muscular as he traveled. He believed God and, therefore, got on the road. True. But once on the road his faith continued to grow.

In other words, belief prompts action, *but action also gives birth to belief*. It's true that people who really believe act in a certain way. It's also true that people who act in a certain way grow in faith. In performance, faith mysteriously blooms. Contrary to our analytical way of thinking about it (which has inspired centuries of futile debate among Christians), then, faith and action are not always sequential (in just one direction) or isolable, but aspects of a single mysterious reality. The Apostle Paul has a phrase for this symbiosis; he calls it "the obedience of faith" (Romans 1:5; 16:26). This is an obedience that gives birth to faith; this is a faith that finds authenticity in action. It is, of course, how most people become disciples.

Years before I committed my life to Christ, I was immersed in particular, faith-building practices—reading the Bible, praying, singing, serving others, worshiping with family members and others, and watching others perform similar practices. In sum, practice came first in my life, long before I "believed." So, where along the way did I become a believer? It's hard to say, except that somewhere in the very observances of the faith, I came to believe what my heart and my body had taught me. "The road to holiness necessarily passes through the world of action," said Dag Hammarskjöld.[6] With the minister narrator in the novel *Gilead*, I discovered "the gift of physical particularity and how blessing and sacrament are mediated through it." I came to love "my physical life."[7]

To say this differently, the spiritual life is also a physical life. Because God created the earth and pronounced it good, and because the Son of God became flesh, we must forever respect and revere material creation. As Nobel poet Czeslaw Milosz wrote, if God became a man, died, and rose from the dead, then:

> All human endeavors deserve attention
> Only to the degree that they depend on this,
> I.e., acquire meaning thanks to this event.
> We should think of this by day and by night.
> Every day, for years, ever stronger and deeper.
> And most of all about how human history is holy
> And how every deed of ours becomes a part of it,
> Is written down forever, and nothing is ever lost.
> Because our kind was so much elevated
> Priesthood should be our calling
> Even if we do not wear liturgical garments.
> We should publicly testify to the divine glory
> With words, music, dance and every sign.[8]

Jesus came to teach us great truths, certainly, but he also came to embed them in a particular way of life. It follows that the authentic Christian life is profoundly earthy, grounded in humble practices.

Despite our indoctrination, we know from experience that body and soul are not separable. When we are injured, we are not merely hurt where the injury occurs. We are hurt throughout. As Hauerwas explains, "Sickness makes it impossible to avoid the reality of our bodies. When I am sick, I am not a mind with a suffering body; I am the suffering body."[9] When I am discouraged or anxious, my sadness or worry permeates my whole being, not some local corner of my brain. I am an ensouled body, an embodied soul.

THE ORDINARY IS SPIRITUAL TOO

There is great news here. One need not be a scholar to follow Jesus. Often those who are most humble may be most open to the message. While God wants us to use all our gifts in his service, including our intellect (indeed, Christianity has been the engine of great scientific and philosophical inquiry), nevertheless, our intelligence does not automatically advantage us before God. "A little child" shall precede the great philosophers, scholars, and professors of the world into the kingdom of heaven. "Learning Jesus" (Luke Timothy Johnson's fine phrase) is very different from learning algebra or physics.[10] Learning Jesus is more akin to being apprenticed to a ship captain, a painter, a musician, or a stone mason. Sailors, painters, musicians, and stone masons work in particular places with very particular materials and tools. Perhaps we should think of the Christian life as similarly grounded in particulars. When Abraham set out for the Promised Land, he took a particular route. He waded across particular streams, climbed particular hills, and no doubt stubbed his toe on very real stones. The disciples on that first Easter Sunday evening traveled a particular road to a particular town (Emmaus), and they ate real bread and drank real wine with the real, resurrected Lord. And so it is with us. Our path is as real and concrete as that of the first century's disciples.

The way of life taught in Scripture is quintessentially an active pilgrimage towards Jesus, characterized by many daily practices. Ours is a "symphonic piety," as Richard Foster calls it:

> The discovery of God lies in the daily and the ordinary, not in the spectacular and the heroic. If we cannot find God in the routines of home and shop, then we will not find him at all. Ours is to be a symphonic piety in which all the activities of work and play and family and worship and sex

and sleep are the holy habitats of the eternal.[11]

Nicholas Herman of Lorraine, commonly known as Brother Lawrence, expressed a similar outlook, even finding God in the noisy kitchen where he was the cook:

> The time of business does not with me differ from the time of prayer, and in the noise and clatter of my kitchen, while several persons are at the same time calling for different things, I possess God in as great tranquility as if I were upon my knees at the blessed sacrament.[12]

Human bodies, by their very nature, perform an almost infinite number of actions. They breathe, eat, walk, sleep, shout, sing, pray, confess, cry, laugh, talk, listen, and so forth. Each is a part of the journey toward God. The chapters that follow are organized around some of the particular verbs which describe the active nature of authentic Christian spirituality. Let us consider the mysterious, wonderful life of the faithful pilgrim walking towards eternity.

PART TWO

PRACTICES OF
THE PILGRIM HEART

3

EMPTYING: A FRESH BREEZE AS WE LET GO

Everything which God is to use, he first reduces to nothing.
—Søren Kierkegaard

And the way up is the way down, the way forward is the way back.
—T. S. Eliot

When Jesus selected his first messengers, the Twelve Apostles, he told them: "Take nothing for your journey, no staff, nor bag, nor bread, nor money—not even an extra tunic" (Luke 9:3). In brief, they were to travel light. Jesus himself practiced a similar kind of missionary minimalism. (He owned nothing.) Since the founding of Christianity, the followers of Jesus have tried to understand what they are to carry with them as they make the journey through life, some interpreting Jesus' prescription for the Apostles quite literally, taking vows of poverty. Others shared their possessions with members of the community, making sure that everyone's needs were cared for (Acts 2:44-45). Christians through time have been taught the essential virtue of "giving alms" (Matthew 6:1-4; Acts 10:2). Jesus issued sober warnings against greed, the accumulation of wealth for its own sake, or trust in material things. The journey with Jesus towards God requires, in one form or another, an emptying of one's pockets, a casting off of any baggage that might inhibit our free travel towards him. Learning "the downward way," as Henri

Nouwen called it, is one of the greatest of spiritual challenges.

The spirit of "emptying" lies at the very heart of Christianity. Thus, unwillingness to empty one's cupboard, whether literal or spiritual, is a serious impediment to the pilgrim heart finding its way to God. For one thing, God has much to offer us, but if we are already full—of ourselves or the things of this world—then we have no room to receive. Satiation, the state of being overly full or satisfied to excess, is as dangerous to the spiritual life as obesity is to the body. In contrast, emptiness in the form of hunger can be a good thing, if it awakens us to what we lack and prompts us to secure what we need. Just as the hungry are motivated to find food, the poor in spirit are particularly apt to become pilgrims in search of something more. This fact helps explain the essential paradox in the great beatitude: "Blessed are the poor in spirit, for theirs is the kingdom of heaven" (Matthew 5:3). As Mary conveys in her wonderful song, God blesses the lowly, the hungry, and the poor in spirit: "He has...lifted up the lowly; he has filled the hungry with good things, and sent the rich away empty" (Luke 1:52-53).

A great contest is ongoing in our hearts. On the one hand, we want to protect ourselves by surrounding ourselves with more. We want the insulation of material wealth and anything else that promises security in a scary world. We hope seatbelts, airbags, and whatever else we can find will minimize the impact of the shocks and the reckless insecurities of daily life. Yet we also know, in our heart of hearts, that these protections are pitifully inadequate.

There is a better way, the downward way, the way of release and relinquishment. This way of Jesus is counterintuitive, where less is truly more, demonstrated by the lives of saints through the ages. It is the way of Francis of Assisi and Henri Nouwen. It is the way of humility, of death to self, a way that brings life. "Very truly, I tell you, unless a grain of wheat falls into the earth and dies, it remains just a single grain; but if it dies, it bears much fruit. Those who love their life lose it, and those who hate their life in this world will keep it for eternal life" (John 12:24-25).

Those who have carried so much for so long are naturally frightened at the prospect of letting go. But to relinquish one's will, to empty oneself—scary as it may seem—is also the way to joy and freedom. Jesus invites us to try his way, a way that is paradoxical and mysterious. The downward way of self-sacrifice is the fundamental requirement that undergirds and informs all the other practices of Jesus' followers. In fact, one could argue that every spiritual discipline (whether worship, prayer, fasting, or whatever) is but a variation on a single theme—emptying oneself.

THE KENOTIC WAY

The spiritual act of pouring out oneself, of "emptying" the self of its preroga-tives, is sometimes called *kenosis*, from the Greek New Testament word *kenoo* found in Philippians 2:7 where Paul writes that Christ "emptied himself," "poured himself out" or "he made himself nothing." While *kenosis* has many nuances, at its core is the idea of relinquishment of authority, power, or prerogative. Jesus stands as the supreme example of this generous act of humility. Paul sees Jesus' act of becoming a human being and living a simple life of service to others as a supreme and eternal pattern for every pilgrim heart. "Let the same mind be in you that was in Jesus Christ," Paul instructs the disciples, embellishing the idea by quoting an evidently familiar early Christian hymn:

> who, though he was in the form of God,
> did not regard equality with God
> as something to be exploited,
> but emptied himself,
> taking the form of a slave,
> being born in human likeness.
> And being found in human form,
> he humbled himself
> and became obedient to the point of death—
> even death on a cross.
> Therefore God also highly exalted him
> and gave him the name
> that is above every name
> so that at the name of Jesus
> every knee should bend,

> in heaven and on earth and under the earth,
>
> and every tongue should confess
>
> that Jesus Christ is Lord
>
> to the glory of God the Father.

Here we see, in summary, the path of the pilgrim heart towards God—a life of yielding up what one has for the sake of others, radical obedience, a downward descent in humility and service, even to the point of shame, self-sacrifice, and death. George F. R. Ellis defines *kenosis* as:

> a joyous, kind, and loving attitude that is willing to give up selfish desires
>
> and to make sacrifices on behalf of others for the common good and the
>
> glory of God, doing this in a generous and creative way, avoiding the pitfall
>
> of pride, and guided and inspired by the love of God and the gift of grace.[1]

How does one reach such a state of heart and mind? If *kenosis* is the goal of the heart's pilgrimage, then we must fervently meditate on how to reach this primary objective.

March of the Penguins (2005) is a feature-length movie that movingly illustrates the theme of *kenosis* in nature. Luc Jacquet's documentary, filmed on location in Antarctica, reports the extraordinary life-cycle of emperor penguins. These beautiful animals survive in the most extreme climate on earth, enduring one-hundred-miles-per-hour blizzards and temperatures of 70 degrees below zero—and worse. What is most remarkable is the effort these animals exert to preserve their young. In February (autumn in the Southern hemisphere), thousands of these birds emerge from the ocean in order to waddle slowly inland seventy miles to their ancient breeding grounds, far from the relatively safe environment of the ocean and their only source of food. The long journey completed, the birds form monogamous couples, mate, and in about two months produce one egg per couple. In the ferocious cold and in the dark of the Antarctic winter, the mother passes a single egg to the father, who then begins to incubate the egg. The father gingerly balances the egg on his feet and covers the egg with the folds of his stomach—and he does this, without food or water, for two more long, bitterly cold months. If the egg is exposed to the cold for even a few seconds, it freezes and the offspring is lost. Meanwhile the mother makes the long trek back to the ocean to feed.

In all this time as he incubates the egg, the father's body weight diminishes by half as he huddles with thousands of other penguin dads, in an effort to keep warm. Finally, the eggs hatch, the mothers return and take up the feeding and care of the young, while the fathers make the long, slow march to the ocean to feed. Eventually, mother, father, and baby penguin arrive at the ocean one year from the original pilgrimage.

It is not an entirely happy tale. Many of the penguins do not survive the long journeys between the breeding grounds and the ocean. Others die in the waters where predators lurk, yet the cycle of care leading to new life continues as it has for millennia. "This is a love story," the movie's narrator, Morgan Freeman, says. It is that, but it is also a parable of heroic self-sacrifice written into nature. It is difficult to watch *March of the Penguins* and not feel the tug of anthropomorphic kinship and some implicit lesson for humankind. Nature can teach us moral and spiritual lessons, so says Scripture: "Go to the ant, you lazybones; consider its ways, and be wise. Without having any chief or officer or ruler, it prepares its food in summer, and gathers its sustenance in harvest" (Proverbs 6:6-7). Recently, leading scientists like John Polkinghorne suggest that modern discoveries of science are deeply compatible with a Trinitarian understanding of things. With other leading scientists, Polkinghorne maintains that creation itself suggests the kenotic, self-giving nature of God.[2]

The writer of Proverbs, had he known the story of the emperor penguins, might well have written, "Go to the emperor penguin, you selfish soul; consider its ways and be wise. Without example, teacher, or law of the land, it compassionately sacrifices its own well being for its children." These odd and ungainly creatures teach us what we are here to do—to live and die for others. Whether we call the penguins' behavior instinct, nature, or love, their extraordinary care for their young in earth's harshest climate is a picture of something fundamentally true. They illustrate *kenosis* in action.

Learning to empty oneself is the most fundamental lesson in the believer's life and surely the most difficult. It begins early—the day we are born into Christ through baptism, for baptism is a door into a peculiar way of life that involves a daily death to self. "Do you not know that all of us who have been baptized into Christ Jesus were baptized into his death?" (Romans 6:3). Consider Bonhoeffer on this point:

> The cross is there, right from the beginning, [the disciple] has only to pick it up; there is no need for him to go out and look for a cross for himself, no need for him deliberately to run after suffering. Jesus says that every Christian has his own cross waiting for him, a cross destined and appointed by God....As we embark upon discipleship we surrender ourselves to Christ in union with his death—we give over our lives to death. Thus it begins; the cross is not the terrible end to an otherwise god-fearing and happy life, but it meets us at the beginning of our communion with Christ. When Christ calls a man, he bids him come and die.[3]

I seriously doubt that anyone learns this lesson quickly or fully. Rather, it is learned by degrees, painfully, inch by inch. Even if yesterday I acted selflessly, there is absolutely no assurance that I will today. There is no formula for success when it comes to dying to self. It is normally the by-product of other disciplines, choices, and experiences, rather than something we can stalk and seize by the direct approach. It is really the sign of obedience learned over a lifetime. Even Jesus "learned obedience" (Hebrews 5:8).

Christianity is a religion of stunning paradoxes. The first shall be last. The least shall be the greatest. The poor will be rich. But one of the greatest of spiritual paradoxes is the strength to be found in weakness and the power found in submission. *Kenosis* is achieved, not through some superhuman effort on our part, but rather in the opposite direction, in giving up and giving in to God. I recall a particularly troubling time in my life when I was in despair over temptation's power. I recall spending time with a very wise man who said something to me one day that stopped me in my tracks. After listening to me for a long while, he said, "Let go." I felt like a man hanging by a thread, and so his words astonished me. The abyss seemed to open up before me, and I was losing strength fast. Yet my friend said, "Let go." Given the context of our long conversations, I knew he wasn't saying, "Give in to temptation." Nor was he saying, "Quit caring." When he said, "Let go," I heard something strange and intriguing. He was saying, "Quit trying to save yourself. Relinquish the self-assumed role of being in charge of your own life." I took his advice, and an amazing thing happened. I found that I was soon in a better place. Why? I had learned to stop trying to be my own savior. I got quiet. I listened, and I yielded to the God who had the strength to help me.

The Psalmist expressed this principle long ago: "Be still and know that I am God" (Psalms 46:10). *Raphah* ("Be still") is a rich Hebrew word meaning a great deal more than "be quiet" or "quit stirring." It also means "to let go," "to be faint," "to be feeble," "to show oneself slack," "to be weak." Be weak! Be slack! Be in abeyance! Strange counsel, indeed, if seen from the point of view of a do-it-yourself philosophy of life; but in the topsy-turvy world of spiritual realities, human effort can actually get in the way of spiritual growth. The pilgrim heart ceases to direct, order, and control.

Many years later, that young French genius Simone Weil taught me the same principle in her highly unconventional but spiritually wise book, *Waiting for God*. Weil stresses the need to make oneself patiently open to God. She understands the spiritual wisdom of a kind of "passive activity," a kind of humble, patient waiting before God that is the source of spiritual growth. She writes:

> There are people who try to raise their souls like a man continually taking standing jumps in the hopes that, if he jumps higher every day, a time may come when he will no longer fall back but will go right up to the sky. Thus occupied he cannot look at the sky. We cannot take a single step toward heaven. It is not in our power to travel in a vertical direction. If however we look heavenward for a long time, God comes and takes us up. He raises us easily....There is an easiness in salvation which is more difficult to us than all our efforts.[4]

There is much here that can be misunderstood, for Weil often speaks in hyperbole and metaphor. An activist all her life, Weil is certainly not calling for a life of carefree indifference, sloth, or quietism. She is calling for a life of self-renunciation. She invites us to "be still," to desire God passionately with all our hearts, but also to abandon the idolatrous illusion that we can reach God—or any worthwhile aim for that matter—through our own muscular wills.

In my own case, I didn't like the direction I was going. My jumping up and down, in Weil's terms, wasn't really getting me any closer to my destination. So I decided to "be still" and let go. Soon, an uncommon peace flooded my heart, and with it a greater power to resist temptation. I found myself in a different place where I struggled less and felt a renewed sense of joy and hope. Learning to "be still" proved to be a turning point in my life. Ever since, "Be still and know that I am God" has been one of the most encouraging messages in my life. It's true that I often forget the wisdom of Psalm 46:10, but it continues to return to me again and again. I am not in charge. God is.

Henri Nouwen reminds us in many of his books that Jesus chose the downward way, not the way of ascent to power and glory; and every serious follower of Jesus will choose to descend with him (which is to relinquish, to fall, to be faint, to be weak).[5] This is strange counsel, bizarre to many people (including many professed Christians), but it is the path to maturity. Nouwen writes:

> Downward mobility with Jesus goes radically against my inclinations, against the advice of the world surrounding me, and against the culture of which I am a part....Wherever I turn I am confronted with my deep-seated resistance against following Jesus on his way to the cross and my countless ways of avoiding poverty, whether material, intellectual, or emotional. Only Jesus, in whom the fullness of God dwells, could freely and fully choose to be completely poor. I see clearer now that choosing to become poor is choosing to make every part of my journey with Jesus. Becoming truly poor is impossible, but "nothing is impossible to God" (Luke 1:37).[6]

Yet the kenotic way of Jesus is not altogether strange, for it is not only modeled in nature, as we see with the emperor penguins; it is embodied in the lives of ordinary mortals whom we encounter every day. Indeed, most of us have been fortunate enough to have witnessed models of radical humility in our families and in our communities. The contemporary American poet Walt McDonald portrays the "ordinary" *kenosis* of a Depression-era mother, nurse, and friend, whose selflessness was utterly unselfconscious:

> She was a mystery of give and take,
> laid open to strangers and neighbors in need,
> no thought of lawsuits in those innocent days.

She took abuse from people she helped feed
in the Texas depression, who quarreled
and promised to pay her back, but frowned
and walked away when they saw her
after church. Our mother never doubted
evil was merely need in neighbors.
She carried fables with her to the grave,
although she saw her father pistol whipped
for giving a man a ride in winter.
A thousand nights she sat with the aged,
the sick and the dying. At thirty-eight,
she ran bare-footed to save a child,
jerking him up from the screaming mother
and pumping the marble out. Then collapsed in the briars
coming back, had to be helped home by others.
My sister tweezered sixty stickers from her feet.
Mother moaned how thankful she missed them
going over, though dozens stuck to her feet
when she ran to that baby on adrenaline
and faith. She never fathomed how pluck happened
throughout her life, how fast it left her
lovely and flushed, trembling with a funeral fan
in her hand, a comely woman, mother, nurse,
who believed herself simple, submissive, afraid,
not knowing how able she was, how recklessly brave.[7]

This "recklessly brave" woman reminds us that anyone can carry the cross daily (Luke 9:23). *Kenosis* is "writ large" in the lives of countless ordinary people who surround us, as well as in the noble and heroic sacrifices of the great saints through the ages.

The invitation to lose our lives daily for Christ's sake also comes to us through the uninvited, ordinary experiences of daily life—sometimes in the petty disappointments and bitter losses that mount up in our lives. Robert Bellah observes:

> For the deepest truth I have discovered is that if one accepts the loss, if one gives up clinging to what is irretrievably gone, then the nothing which is left is not barren but is enormously fruitful. Everything that one has lost comes flooding back again out of the darkness, and one's relation to it is new—free and unclinging. But the richness of the nothing contains far more, it is the all-possible, it is the spring of freedom. In that sense, the faith of loss is closer to joy than to despair.[8]

Facing and accepting the losses that come with time—diminished physical and mental capacities as we age, lost career opportunities, waning vigor, and broken relationships—are, paradoxically, the way to freedom. They are also the way to Christlikeness.

There are other things we must learn to relinquish as we walk with Jesus. We must relinquish power, the great temptation, even of the devout, perhaps especially of the religiously devout. Nouwen observes:

> We keep hearing from others, as well as saying to ourselves, that having power—provided it is used in the service of God and your fellow human beings—is a good thing. With this rationalization, crusades took place; inquisitions were organized; Indians were enslaved; positions of great influence were desired; episcopal palaces, splendid cathedrals, and opulent seminars were built; and much moral manipulation of conscience was engaged in. Every time we see a major crisis in the history of the Church, such as the Great Schism of the eleventh century, the Reformation of the sixteenth century, or the immense secularization of the twentieth century, we always see that a major cause of rupture is the power exercised by those who claim to be followers of the poor and powerless Jesus. What makes the temptation of power so seemingly irresistible? Maybe it is that power offers an easy substitute for the hard task of love.[9]

One has to marvel at the stunning desolations that have been wrought by Christians' failure to relinquish their inordinate desire for power over others. How many churches have been burdened or splintered by leaders who exerted unquestioned power over their flocks? How many families have been torn asunder by one spouse using his or her authority improperly over the other spouse or the children? How many workplaces have been turned into dens of anguish because a boss or a co-worker exercised coercive power over his or her fellow workers? *Kenosis* is an antidote to such cruel abuses. Humbling oneself, forgiving others, renouncing one's own inflated certainty (abandoning the fatal need to be right about everything), sharing our material goods, receiving criticism in humility, saying "I'm sorry," resisting our need to be first, renouncing our "rights," our entitlements, and our prerogatives—we must practice such daily "deaths" of the self over and over again if we are to develop our pilgrim hearts.

However, it should be reiterated: Being formed in the image of Jesus is not our doing. It is God's mysterious, miraculous work in our lives. It's really much more about getting out of the way so that God is free to work within us. When New Testament writers describe the process of becoming like Jesus, they do so using passive verbs. The process is done to us. It is not something we ourselves do. Thus, Paul says that we are "conformed" to "the image of God's Son" (Romans 8:29). (We do not conform ourselves. God does the crafting.) As we look to Jesus, we "are *being transformed* into the same image from one degree of glory to another; *for this comes from the Lord, the Spirit*" (2 Corinthians 3:18, my emphasis). By gazing on Christ and by refusing to be in charge, God's Spirit slowly fashions us into the image of the Son. (The most we can do is quiet our own wills, so that his will can be effective within us.) Finally, we rest, knowing it is God's creative energy that leads the pilgrim heart towards God: "For we are what he made us, created in Christ Jesus for good works, which God prepared beforehand to be our way of life" (Ephesians 2:10).

CAVEAT: ON FALSE *KENOSIS*

The downward way of *kenosis* is a central theme of Christianity, yet it is a teaching that is subject to distortion and abuse. *Kenosis* requires the relinquishment of power and privilege; yet, ironically and tragically, this sacred principle has been used as a tool to control others. Rather than serving as a call to all believers to "regard others better than yourselves" (Philippians 2:3), some men have been able to manipulate and control women by narrowing the application of the principle. Miroslav Volf has shrewdly noted, "Giving was what women, as mothers and wives, were supposed to do so that men, as sons and husbands, could do all the taking."[10] Thus, *kenosis* became "gendered" in ways never taught in Scripture. Women were to be self-giving, but men were not. Such thinking mocks Scripture, which calls for mutual submission (Ephesians 5:21), "reciprocal self-donation" (Volf's term), the renunciation of selfish ambition and conceit by every follower of Jesus (Philippians 2:3). If *kenosis* becomes a tool of exploitation of the weak, then what Jesus taught and practiced has been nullified.

At times kenotic behavior has been viewed as a rare spiritual gift appropriate only for church professionals, or for those who adopted extreme, ascetic lives of service (such as members of monastic orders). Meanwhile, the rest of the Christian church was mostly excused. Applying *kenosis* only to the spiritually elite also eviscerates the gospel and renders meaningless Jesus' explicit teaching that every disciple must take up the cross and follow him daily. Such a view is just another version of the "cheap grace" exposed by Bonhoeffer in *The Cost of Discipleship*.

Still others misread *kenosis* to mean that devout Christians should be people without strength of character, moral resolve, or bold ideas. They misconstrue *kenosis* to teach that followers of Jesus should be happy doormats for any heavy-handed bully in the neighborhood. Nothing could be further from the truth. We need only look at Jesus. One can be meek and gentle, like Jesus, "[doing] nothing from selfish ambition or conceit, but in humility regard[ing] others as better than yourselves," (Philippians 2:3), without abandoning one's values, and without yielding to "enmeshment" or coercive power brokers. Jesus teaches us how *kenosis* is to work. He is meek and lowly, the humble servant to the weak, the needy, and the outcast. He also confronted evil bravely. He taught us to be wise as serpents, as well as harmless as doves.

A great deal of reflection and prayer about the true nature of humility is in order. Humility before others is essential, but it doesn't follow that we yield ourselves automatically to those who are abusive and who have evil intentions. When is it appropriate to resist wrong-doing? When must we wait patiently and bear the slings and arrows of outrageous fortune? Immersion in the life of Jesus and in the life of the community helps a great deal to answer such questions. *Kenosis* requires something of us that is strangely countercultural, rare, and little understood. It is a practice to be learned in community over time, practiced in tandem with the essential spiritual practices of listening and discernment.

4

WELCOMING: OPENING DOORS TO STRANGERS

"Welcome one another, therefore, as Christ has welcomed you,
for the glory of God."
Romans 15:7

"I was a stranger and you welcomed me."
Matthew 25:35

Melania, Marcella, Paula, Eustochium, and Olympias. If our knowledge of Christian history were better, we would know the full stories of these women, and we would celebrate their efforts which helped to make Christianity the world religion that it is today. It was not only the preaching of the early missionaries that led millions to the faith during the first three centuries of the Christian era. Equally important was the radical hospitality practiced by Benedict of Nursia, Basil (bishop of Caesarea), John Chrysostom, and many other disciples who remain nameless.[1] The notion of loving the stranger, no matter the cost, revolutionized the cultures of Europe and changed human history forever.

The earliest Christians were often exhorted to care for strangers: "Extend hospitality to strangers," Paul taught the Roman Christians (Romans 12:13). "Do not neglect to show hospitality to strangers," the disciples were told (Hebrews 13:2). Aspiring church leaders were expected to demonstrate their worthiness to lead the flock through their exemplary practice of hospitality (1 Timothy 3:2; Titus 1:8). According to social historian Rodney Stark, the revolutionary practice of hospitality helps to explain why the tiny Jesus movement became the dominant religion of the Western world by the fourth century.[2] To understand Christian faith one must see that the gracious treatment of strangers is foundational.

Welcoming strangers is a frequent and significant practice in the Old Testament, and the first Christians carefully considered this fact. Abraham, the "father of all who believe," welcomes three strangers out of the noonday heat into his home. These visitors, who receive Abraham's generous courtesies of refreshment, prove to be divine messengers who bring Abraham and Sarah a blessing, prophesying that they will be parents (Genesis 18). This ancient scene presents an archetypal pattern often repeated throughout Scripture and Christian history: a needy stranger unexpectedly appears; the believer spontaneously and graciously receives the guest or guests; the visitor in turn brings a blessing to the host; finally, in retrospect, if not immediately, the meeting proves to be sacred. In the encounter there is discovery, epiphany, an experience of the sacred. This is the experience of the disciples in Emmaus who invite a stranger to their table: "Then they told what had happened on the road, and how he had been made known to them in the breaking of the bread" (Luke 24:35). When you welcome strangers, according to the Bible, you may be entertaining cosmic messengers, perhaps God himself (Genesis 18; Hebrews 13:2; Matthew 25:35). This understanding of hospitality has powerfully motivated Christian service through the centuries.

The Hebrew people, having experienced brutal oppression in an alien land, were taught to treat the strangers in their midst with generous respect. From early in their history they knew that the Lord God "loves the strangers" (Deuteronomy 10:17-19). Therefore, "[y]ou shall not oppress a resident alien; you know the heart of an alien, for you were aliens in the land of Egypt" (Exodus 23:9). Sympathy and identity with the stranger in one's own community was a recurring theme of the Old Testament, and it proved to be a central theme of Jesus' teaching and practice. The idea of hospitality circulates through his stories as in the parable of the Good Samaritan, and in his generous treatment of the lowest, most invisible members of society. Jesus consistently acted out of a concern for those on the margins in tangible ways and to such a degree that it made him a scandal to those most concerned with ritual purity.

LOVING THOSE OUTSIDE THE NEIGHBORHOOD

While Jesus affirmed the ancient Hebrew understanding of hospitality, he also adapted the concept, enlarging the definition of neighbor. One's neighbor is not only the alien dwelling in one's own village, but the stranger far afield—beyond one's immediate community. An unprecedented love of all humankind permeated Jesus' teaching and practice, and his first followers caught the spirit of it. The pilgrim heart journeys far beyond the comfort zone of one's own neighborhood or social group:

> When you give a luncheon or a dinner, do not invite your friends or your brothers or your relatives or your rich neighbors, in case they may invite you in return, and you would be repaid. But when you give a banquet, invite the poor, the crippled, the lame, and the blind. And you will be blessed because they cannot repay you, for you will be repaid at the resurrection of the righteous. (Luke 14:12-14)

According to the way of Jesus, hospitality does not concern fine linens, elegant crystal, or gourmet cooking. Rather, it consists of a generous heart and a welcoming spirit that leads to tangible expressions of care for others. Very importantly, it entails an active concern for those different from ourselves. The English word "hospitality" does not quite capture the meaning of the Greek word used in the New Testament. *Philoxenia* actually suggests loving foreigners or aliens. This is a challenging, paradoxical love: a kinship, friendship love extended to a stranger, someone not related or known to us. No one before Jesus had taken hospitality this far, but the early Christians became inflamed with the spirit of *philoxenia*, and this radical love of those on the margins (the sick, the hungry, the homeless, destitute widows, wayfarers) took the ancient world by storm. The evidence of its radical power is documented by the church fathers and historians of the ancient world.[3]

CHRISTIANITY'S GROWTH THROUGH HOSPITALITY

The significance of Jesus' kind of hospitality is considerable when seen against the dark canvas of the ancient world. Life was risky and ever fraught with danger. Catastrophic plagues raged through Europe, especially in A.D. 165 and 260, killing hundreds of thousands, perhaps millions. At the height of one epidemic 5,000 people a day were dying in Rome. Two-thirds of Alexandria's population was wiped out.[4] Life in the Roman Empire teetered on the edge of disaster. Risking their lives by the thousands, compassionate disciples waded into this horrific maelstrom of death, ministering to the sick and dying in the name of Christ. Remarkably, they tended to dying pagans as well as to their own; and the shocked but desperate pagans took notice. According to Dionysius, the bishop of Alexandria: "Heedless of danger, [the Christians] took charge of the sick, attending to their every need and ministering to them in Christ, and with them departed this life serenely happy...."[5] Once the plague had passed, countless survivors owed their lives to Jesus' followers who had nursed them. The survivors were never the same again, and the church flourished because of this exceptional hospitality to the sick.

Hospitality took new forms in the ensuing centuries. Throughout the ancient and medieval worlds Christians established "hospitals" (*xenodochia*, 'guest-houses'), not institutions exclusively for the sick according to the modern sense of the term, but houses of care for people with varying needs: widows, orphans, strangers, the poor, travelers, as well as the sick. Originally "hospital" (Latin *hospitalia*) signified any place of reception for a guest, whether pilgrim, invalid, or needy stranger. These richly varied practices of caring for strangers can still be traced through the related English words *hospital, hospice, hotel, hostel, hospitality, host,* and *hostess*. The unbelieving world had never seen anything like this kind of nonsectarian concern, and it astonished them. Not only did they say of the Christians, "Only look! See how they love one another!"[6] But they must have marveled and said to themselves, "Look! See how they love us, who are not of their faith!"

A wealthy Roman matron named Fabiola, who died in 399, established the first (medical) hospital in the Western world. With one Pammachius she also established homes for the destitute and a guest-house for travelers and pilgrims visiting Rome.[7] Congregations established ambitious missions to the poor. The church in Antioch, for example, fed three thousand destitute widows and virgins daily, in addition to caring for prisoners, the sick, the disabled, and travelers. The breadth of Christian care in the ancient world is startling and inspiring. According to Rodney Stark:

...Christianity revitalized life in Greco-Roman cities by providing new norms and new kinds of social relationships able to cope with many urgent urban problems. To cities filled with the homeless and impoverished, Christianity offered charity as well as hope. To cities filled with newcomers and strangers, Christianity offered an immediate basis for attachments. To cities filled with orphans and widows, Christianity provided a new and expanded sense of family. To cities torn by violent ethnic strife, Christianity offered a new basis for social solidarity....And to cities faced with epidemics, fires, and earthquakes, Christianity offered effective nursing services.[8]

Hospitality of this kind continues today, mostly through great institutions that have either secularized the care (e.g., the Red Cross, Doctors Without Borders, government-funded medical centers, philanthropic foundations) or through large, complex faith-based charities (e.g., the Salvation Army, World Vision, Habitat for Humanity, etc.). One can be thankful that Christian understandings of charity have permeated international organizations and whole societies.

GOSPEL HOSPITALITY RECONSIDERED

While we can be grateful for this legacy, the notion of hospitality as *a personal and collective discipline in the life of the believer and the church* must be renewed in our time. If we do not personally feel the urgent call to love the stranger, if our own hands do not touch the sick, the poor, the dying, can we really say that we are walking with Abraham or Jesus? Jesus speaks these simple words in our ears each day, *"I was a stranger and you took me in."* He modeled specific, tactile forms of care that challenge us all; and we should be restless until we offer back to him—in the persona of the stranger—a bed, a cup of cold water, and a healing touch.

The pilgrim heart understands that long-distance care is necessary, but not sufficient. The first disciples in the Roman Empire took up collections for Jewish believers in far-away Jerusalem, but they also ministered to those close to home. In later years church treasuries grew. When some Christians felt less obligation to provide personal care to others, Chrysostom cajoled them to reconsider. Even if a needy person could be cared for by church funds, he asked: "Can that benefit you?

If another man prays, does it follow that you are not bound to pray?"[9] Basil the Great preached:

> The bread in your cupboard belongs to the hungry person; the coat hanging unused in your closet belongs to the person who needs it; the shoes rotting in your closet belong to the person with no shoes; the money which you put in the bank belongs to the poor. You do wrong to everyone you could help, but fail to help.[10]

Institutional hospitality, in other words, was no substitute for the individual's personal obligation.

So how do we practice the radical hospitality of Jesus? Rather than try to motivate ourselves to good deeds through blame and shame, we might do two things. First, we could meditate on Jesus' extraordinary hospitality towards us, experiencing afresh what "being at home" with Jesus is like. Since we were first welcomed by Jesus in our deepest need, while we were profoundly unworthy and alienated, what can we do but gratefully respond in kind? When we consider that, despite our shame and unworthiness, we were welcomed by Christ, that we were invited to sit at his table and taste his food and that we were offered lavish attention and radical forgiveness, shouldn't it come to us naturally to want to return the favor by treating others with an analogous generosity? Second, we can learn from the hospitality of the exceptional hosts and hostesses who surround us. The saints who preceded us and the saints who live among us today have much to teach us about the spirit of welcome. Many exemplars of hospitality have welcomed me across their threshold through the years, and I shall conclude this chapter by describing one in particular who has taught me the meaning of gospel welcome.

THE "HOMELY" JESUS

Most of my life I have imagined Jesus as a kind of homeless person, perhaps because he said: "Foxes have holes, and birds of the air have nests; but the Son of Man has nowhere to lay his head" (Matthew 8:20). Thus, in my thinking, Jesus sometimes has floated above the earth a bit, without pillow or bedroom or couch. Yet I am not so sure that we should picture Jesus as homeless in quite that way. The point of Matthew 8:20 seems to be not that Jesus was a street person (he did have a place to stay, as John 1:39 and other texts suggest), but rather that the nature of his residence was extraordinary. In fact, Jesus invites us to "abide" with him—not in a particular house on a certain street in Capernaum or Bethany—but in a place nonetheless. Jesus is himself our "home." He is the embodiment of home. Indeed, if we welcome him into our lives, our home becomes his dwelling, and his ours.

When the first two disciples (Andrew and another unnamed follower) encounter Jesus, he asks them, *"What are you looking for?"* And they reply, curiously, with their own question: *"Where are you staying?"* To their question, the Master replies, *"Come and see."* Andrew and his friend follow Jesus to his lodging, "and they remained with him that day" (John 1:35-42, my emphasis). This anecdote reveals more than meets the eye, for to "remain," in John's language, is to abide or commune with Jesus, to share a common life with him. To remain with Jesus is to enjoy hospitality. When you follow Jesus, you find your true home. Thus, in John's gospel Jesus' ministry begins and ends with Jesus extending gracious hospitality. Many word pictures describe the Messiah of the New Testament, but one is often overlooked: "Gracious Host."

One extraordinary English writer has helped me discover this often overlooked dimension to Jesus. Lady Julian of Norwich was a fourteenth-century anchoress, which is to say that she was a recluse who offered spiritual counsel to members of the Norwich congregation and to others who traveled long distances to learn from her. On May 13, 1373, at age thirty, Lady Julian fell seriously ill. She lost her eyesight and all feeling, and she nearly died. During this traumatic ordeal she experienced a series of "shewings" or visions. She eventually recovered and spent the rest of her life trying to grasp the meaning of these near-death experiences. She apparently dictated and then revised an account of this life-changing ordeal, producing the first book in the English language composed by a woman. Though many of her reflections are strange and uncanny, her *Revelations of Divine Love* is considered a classic of Christian spirituality and a source of considerable insight.

One of Julian's insights seems very much "at home" with what the Gospel writers convey, namely, that meeting Jesus is both amazing ("dreadful" is Julian's medieval word), but also "homely." Whatever really happened to Julian during her grave illness, she derived from it an absolute conviction of the greatness of God's love. Christ was to her "a solemn king," a great and noble lord; but, like a mother towards her children, he was also humble and accessible, intimate and tender towards his creatures. The word she used over and over for Christ's demeanor towards his followers was "homely." Christ, she wrote, is "so homely and so courteous." Julian says that she was ravished by his "marvelous homeliness."

In Julian's day, "homely" did not mean "plain-featured" or "unattractive." (That definition developed centuries later.) In her day, "homely" meant "intimate," "familiar," "established on a friendly footing," or "homey." Curiously, this meaning is preserved in German and in Yiddish today. The German *heimisch* can mean homey, native, or local (as opposed to foreign). A Jewish friend once tried to convey to me her pleasure at working alongside her Christian colleagues. As she searched for the right word, she settled on *heymish*, a Yiddish term meaning "domestic, cozy, familiar, intimate," to describe her sense of at-homeness with her colleagues.

Heymish, heimisch, homely—the first followers of Jesus, like Lady Julian, found him "at home" through a deeply affirming welcome, and so can we. While we have not had Lady Julian's particular experience, we can know the same Lord who comes to our house just like he did to Zaccheus's. There is an easy familiarity with the master of the universe that boggles the imagination. Jesus addressed God familiarly, one might say "heimishly" as "Abba," the intimate Aramaic name for one's father (Mark 14:36).[11] It is possible to meet the Lord Jesus and the Master of the Universe on such intimate terms, to experience a brotherly and fatherly embrace, and, in turn, to practice a similarly radical hospitality towards others.

NOUWEN'S "FREE AND FRIENDLY SPACE"

I hate to admit it, but I heard the Good News preached and taught for many years before I took seriously the revolutionary nature of Christ's welcome. While my outward demeanor towards strangers was decent enough, I harbored suspicions of those who were different from me, especially if they were theologically different from me. A surface gentility masked an inward fear or dislike. In time, though, I learned a great deal about the grace of hospitality from those outside my own faith tradition. Believers from other communions modeled a gracious welcome towards me that brought me up short, exposing my own anemic understanding of hospitality.

The first major challenge came in the summer of my sophomore year in college. I was living in Ohio, far from home, and working in a town that had no congregation of my tradition. While there, I met the minister of another church. Despite our differences, he welcomed me effusively and then invited me to preach in his congregation. I can still recall my surprise at this invitation. We hardly knew each another, but he welcomed me as a brother and offered me his pulpit on a Sunday night. I couldn't refuse, and so, as a young man of twenty, I preached my first full sermon in a church outside my own communion. That experience caused the first crack in my youthful sectarianism. Through the years, I have met and been befriended by believers from many different churches. Perhaps the most remarkable experience of hospitality came from the Catholic priest Henri Nouwen, whom I met three times. The first time was at a conference on faith and the arts held at the Graduate Theological Union in Berkeley. At the first session I sat alone, for I didn't know anyone there. Just before the program began, Nouwen walked over and introduced himself to me. His friendly spirit and the fact that he initiated the conversation surprised and humbled me.

A few years later, he agreed to my request for an interview for an article about his work. I met him on a bitterly cold December day, just after Christmas, at Daybreak, the L'Arche community outside Toronto. Nouwen's warmth was the antithesis of that cold day, and it became a vivid example of the L'Arche community's philosophy that the home should be a true *foyer* (originally Latin for "hearth" or "fireplace"). This meeting of strangers turned into a remarkable time of hospitality. Despite the fact that Nouwen was leaving that evening for Europe for an extended visit, our conversation was leisurely, and it went beyond the appointed time. He took me into a small library off his study, gathered copies of his books that I didn't already own, inscribed them, and gave them to me. He then took me to lunch at a favorite local restaurant in Richmond Hill. Over lunch, we talked about many things. Why did Henri spend this time with me? If you read his books, you will know, for to Henri hospitality is the gospel.

Henri Nouwen illustrated to me how one can warmly welcome someone without relinquishing one's convictions. It was clear to Henri that I was not Catholic, but our theological differences did not hamper his capacity to offer me gracious attention. In his books one can find the motivation for Henri's remarkable openness to strangers. Hospitality, he wrote, is "the creation of a free and friendly space where we can reach out to strangers and invite them to become our friends."[12] That day in the Daybreak community, the warm spirit of gospel welcome was enfleshed in this tall, quiet, self-effacing Dutch priest. My encounters, first with Nouwen's books and then with him personally, have caused me to reevaluate my own capacity to reach out to others. How do I receive those who are different from me? Do I generously welcome those who are not altogether upright or theologically tidy? Jesus welcomed me "just as I am." Dare I do the same?

Someone may wonder: Can one welcome those with whom one disagrees theologically or morally without being tainted in some way? Of course, Jesus' critics felt the very same concerns: "And the Pharisees and the scribes were grumbling and saying, 'This fellow welcomes sinners and eats with them'" (Luke 15:2). Perhaps we should just admit it: gospel hospitality is necessarily "dangerous" and capable of being misunderstood. So be it. Jesus welcomed others to his table without compromising his standards, and so can we.

I have come to see that extending a heartfelt welcome does not require one to alter one's convictions or abandon one's practices, though in the encounter either participant may well be changed, for the encounter involves the presence of Christ; and when Christ is present, change occurs. Henri taught me this:

> We become beautiful people when we give whatever we can give: a smile, a
> handshake, a kiss, an embrace, a word of love, a present, a part of our life...
> all of our life....It is sad that, in our highly competitive and greedy world,
> we have lost touch with the joy of giving. We often live as if our happiness
> depended on having. But I don't know anyone who is really happy because
> of what he or she has. True joy, happiness and inner peace come from
> giving of ourselves to others. A happy life is a life for others.[13]

I realize that I have far to go on the journey towards being a truly hospitable host.

In this multicultural world, so far removed from that homogeneous village of my childhood, I constantly meet Christians of all kinds, as well as Jews, Muslims, and secularists. How do I love them with the love of Jesus? I don't have all the answers, but I have Jesus as my model and two thousand years of witnesses to teach me. I remember Olympia and Chrysostom, Basil and Benedict, Lady Julian and Henri Nouwen—and I know that, through the indwelling power of God's Spirit, I can be like my Master, who is both guest and host wherever I go. I do know my calling: to welcome strangers, all those people who cross my path who do not belong to my family, race, or nation (as well as those who do).

In practicing the discipline of welcome, we do not reduce Christianity either to a naïve moralism or a burdensome system of salvation by works. Extending hospitality is the sacred privilege of those who have already been redeemed. Precisely because we have already received unimaginable, unmerited grace (grace being but another name for divine hospitality), we imitate our Savior by opening our homes, our lives, our checkbooks, and our hearts to others. Like the saintly widows noted by the Apostle Paul, all followers of Jesus should be devoted "to doing good in every way" (1 Timothy 5:9-10). There is no more essential spiritual practice than hospitality. Menno Simons, the sixteenth-century Anabaptist, wrote in 1539: "True evangelical faith cannot lie dormant."

> It clothes the naked.
> It feeds the hungry.
> It comforts the sorrowful.
> It shelters the destitute.
> It serves those that harm it.
> It binds up that which is wounded....

5

RESTING: THE DAY
SABBATH BECOMES JOY

For everything there is a season,
and a time for every matter under heaven.
Ecclesiastes 3:1

Work is not always required of man. There is such a thing
as sacred idleness, the cultivation of which is now fearfully neglected.
—George MacDonald

Rhythm. Rhythm lies at the core of all existence—natural and human. Rhythm is
seen in sunrise and sunset, in the patterns of the waves crashing on the seashore, in the
cycles of the seasons (seedtime, harvest, and fallow), the migration patterns of birds
and butterflies, and in the circadian rhythms of countless species. Rhythm is found in
our breathing and our heartbeats; it is basic to music and all the arts—poetry, fiction,
film, dance, and painting. Rhythm not only makes life interesting; it makes life possible.

Yet many today are going to great lengths to defy these innate, God-ordained
patterns. The challenges to these natural rhythms are so pervasive that we hardly
notice them, even when the consequences are large. Consider, for example, our
obliteration of the distinction between day and night. On a clear night one should
see 2,500 stars and a luminous Milky Way; however, because electric lights wash out
the night sky, in a typical suburb one can see barely see 250 stars, and the Milky
Way is invisible. In midtown Manhattan one might only see about 15 stars.[1] Some
city children have never seen a falling star, picked out a constellation, or been

mystified by the Milky Way. Perhaps there is no tragedy in the loss of such visual wonders, but a great deal more is at stake than a blank sky, as we shall see.

As time passes, an ever smaller remnant of the population is even aware of the agricultural calendar. We expect the same foodstuffs to fill our supermarkets twelve months out of the year regardless of drought, flood, blight, or winter. Thanks to technology and imported foods that arrive from thousands of miles away, peaches and watermelon and nearly anything else we could want are always in season. All of this is wonderful—to a point. What happens when we alienate ourselves from nature and our own bodies? What becomes of body and soul when we overthrow the natural order of things?

Many are finding out through seasons of insomnia, exhaustion, and depression. Paradoxically, our abundance leads to a dull joylessness which settles over us and empties us of life. A rhythmless life may be making us sick, and it could even kill us. According to various studies, disruption of our circadian rhythms may influence cancer progression. Various scientific studies suggest that artificial light increases the risk of cancer.[2] Psychological, physical, and spiritual ills may be the consequence of our rhythmless lives. But it doesn't have to be this way. This may be a case in which we have grown less intelligent as we have become more technologically sophisticated.

In recent years, my wife and I have enjoyed hosting a number of interesting house guests. One of them was an eighty-year-old Orthodox rabbi from Brooklyn. He stayed with us so that he could attend a weekend seminar, which was being conducted a short walk from our house. By staying with us, he could avoid driving his car and thus keep the Sabbath. Rabbi David enjoyed a very quiet Friday evening and Saturday in our home. Given our busy, overly scheduled Saturday, David's quiet presence among us was a reminder of what we did not have—*shalom*. His way of life stood as a kind of silent witness against our frenzied busyness. At the end of our weekend, I wondered: who enjoys the healthier life?

My aim is not to propose that we adopt some burdensome set of sabbatarian rules. However, I do believe there are principles in Sabbath-keeping that transcend the Jewish law and apply broadly to all spiritually minded people. Jesus honored the Sabbath, and his followers should try to understand why. Because on occasion Jesus violated the strict rules of the Sabbath, his followers have sometimes misunder-stood his intent in doing so. Jesus rejected a joyless, legalistic interpretation of the Sabbath, one that viewed Sabbath-keeping in rigid and even inhumane terms. For many in Jesus' day, Sabbath was not about liberating rest, but law and proscription. Yet there is another view of Sabbath that runs through Scripture: Sabbath as gracious permission, a blessed and humane gift, the liberty of rest. Jewish slaves enjoyed no Sabbath in Egypt since rest is the privilege of liberated people. Jesus' words should be received as extravagant good news: "The sabbath was made for humankind, and not humankind for the sabbath; so the Son of Man is lord even of the sabbath" (Mark 2:27-28). It is this positive understanding of Sabbath as a wonderful benefit and blessing to humanity that our culture greatly needs. Sabbath—which I use broadly to signify rest, "down time," quiet, renewal, recreation, getting away—can occur any day of the week. It can be even a part of a busy day.[3]

One way to understand the blessing of rest in a culture that does not much appreciate it is to approach it indirectly through a series of beatitudes or blessings. Some of Jesus' most famous beatitudes are paradoxical and counterintuitive in nature: "Blessed are the poor in spirit," "Blessed are those who mourn...," "Blessed are you when people revile you and persecute you..." (Matthew 5:3, 4, 11). Why paradox? If the world is topsy-turvy, then you have to challenge people's notions of what is "normal" or rational. As A. N. Wilson has put it, "If the world itself is inverted, then the only way to see it clearly is upside down. If the values of the world are the wrong way round, then the only way to wisdom is to stand those values on their head."[4] As Jesus looks at his harried and hurried disciples today, one can imagine what he would say about our frenzied lives. I can't help thinking that he might pronounce some paradoxical blessings—or beatitudes—like the following.

BEATITUDE FOR OUR TIME NO. 1:
"HAPPY ARE THOSE WHO SERVE THE WORLD BY ABANDONING IT FOR A LITTLE WHILE."

Or perhaps he would say, "Blessed are those who disappear for a while in order to be fully present," or "Blessed are those who enter silence, for they will hear God."

As Scripture and millennia of spiritual wisdom teach us, retreat from the world is one of the best ways to serve others. Times set apart for silence, reflection, prayer, and other forms of worship can permanently change our understanding of our mission and our relationship to the world. It is remarkable how often the great teachers in the Bible spent time in desert places—Moses, Elijah, John the Baptist, Paul, and, of course, Jesus. For Americans taught to be as productive as possible, time in the desert (unless it is very brief) seems irresponsible. Yet the Desert Fathers and the monastics have a great deal to teach us about true "productivity." Thomas Merton once observed that retreat helps us "recuperate spiritual powers that may have been gravely damaged by the noise and rush of a pressurized existence....Not all men [or women] are called to be hermits, but all...need enough silence and solitude in their lives to enable the deep inner voice of their own true self to be heard at least occasionally."[5]

The reluctance to retreat arises in part from the often unspoken suspicion that such an activity is selfish or, even worse, an irresponsible abandonment of one's duty to the world. While the desire to escape responsibility could drive someone to retreat, for many others retreat is about finding one's calling and allowing fresh breezes to fill one's sails. Thomas Merton argues that a life continuously immersed in society may be more spiritually dangerous than the supposed escapism of retreat. In actuality, immersion in society may be an awful form of escape:

> True solitude is the home of the person, false solitude the refuge of the individualist. The person is constituted by a uniquely subsisting capacity to love—by a radical ability to care for all beings made by God and loved by Him. Such a capacity is destroyed by the loss of perspective. Without a certain element of solitude there can be no compassion because when a man is lost in the wheels of a social machine he is no longer aware of human needs as a matter of personal responsibility. One can escape from men by plunging into the midst of a crowd.[6]

So, Merton, advises, "Go into the desert not to escape other men but in order to find them in God." As he sees it, solitude is not abandonment of the world, but a way to silence the distracting chatter that leads to compassionate insight: "The constant din of empty words and machine noises, the endless booming of loudspeakers end by making true communication and true communion almost impossible. Each individual...doesn't care, he doesn't hear, he doesn't think."[7]

The saints, by contrast, are the ones who are "sanctified," that is, set apart, not because they are superior to others (for they are not). According to Merton, "Their sanctity is given to them in order that they may help us and serve us—for the saints are like doctors and nurses who are better than the sick in the sense that they are healthy and possess arts of healing them, and yet they make themselves the servants of the sick and devote their own health and art to them."[8] One sees the truth of Merton's insights in the lives of the great followers of Jesus through the centuries. Francis of Assisi, for example, built two dozen hermitages so that he and his brothers could retreat and rest, but he built these retreat centers near cities and town in order that the brothers could easily serve the people. Like the Franciscans, every follower of Jesus needs a place of retreat. We have to challenge the dubious assumption that our world or our work will fall to chaos without our constant presence and control.

Before visiting Henri Nouwen in 1993, I asked some friends if they had any questions they would like me to pose to him. A mother with young children asked me to relay this question: How can parents with small children practice the spiritual disciplines? She was asking if the spiritual life that Nouwen recommended was an unattainable ideal for families with children and only for those—like Nouwen—who were single and childless. Could a life of retreat really be possible for the soccer mom or a father with a business and a long commute to work? Of all the topics Nouwen addressed during my time with him, he devoted the greatest attention to this one. Rather than see children and their care as an impediment to one's spiritual vocation, Nouwen stressed the importance of including the children in one's call to retreat: "solitude is an essential element for the spiritual health of a child," he told me:

> If we only stimulate our children—keep them busy with endless stories with
> no space to be alone—that's not good. A sense of solitude is one of the most
> beautiful things that parents can give a child. It doesn't mean leaving the

child alone, but it does mean creating safe spaces where the child can be
with other people. It does mean directing their attention to God.[9]
Nouwen offered a great deal of helpful advice about how to create a home with a certain
atmosphere, making mealtimes an occasion for community. He emphasized the
necessity of ritualizing the dinner table, turning off the television and the telephones.
"Solitude, community, and ministry are certainly not just for celibates!" he insisted.

I came to see that Nouwen's spirituality was not as otherworldly as many have
supposed. He lived in a very noisy and demanding household. In fact, the challenges
to his solitude were far greater than any I have known as a husband and father, for
Nouwen lived in a home with severely handicapped adults who required laborious
attention. At Daybreak he spent hours washing, dressing, and feeding Adam
Arnett, a severely handicapped man. Rather than detracting from Nouwen's
spiritual life, Adam became a powerful vehicle for it. In other words, Nouwen lived
daily the kind of life he had told me it was possible for families to live. Later, he
wrote a book about Adam, in which he said:

> Being so close to Adam I realized that the "Christ event" is much more than
> something that took place long ago. It occurs every time spirit greets spirit
> in the body. It is a sacred event happening in the present because it is God's
> event among people. This is what the sacramental life is all about. It is God's
> on-going incarnation whenever people meet each other "in God's name."[10]

In the loving care Nouwen gave Adam each day, Nouwen found himself encountering
God. Thus, what might have been a distraction became a vehicle of the divine presence.

Personal circumstances vary greatly, of course. Each must find a way to enter
Sabbath rest. It may be found in the earliest hours of the day (as Jesus found it—
Mark 1:35) or late at night after the children are tucked in bed. Finding time may
mean that one must forego an optional task or an assignment at work. It may mean
practicing short retreats at times—five minutes between tasks; a lunch hour devoted
to quiet, prayer or meditation; or a short walk in the park alone with God. There are
ways to take the most routine and obligatory tasks and transform them into small
retreats. (My wife quotes Brother Lawrence occasionally: "To cook is to pray.")
Wherever we find ourselves, the need for retreat remains constant.

BEATITUDE FOR OUR TIME NO. 2:
"HAPPY ARE THOSE WHO REST, FOR THEY WILL GET THEIR WORK DONE."

In the Jewish reckoning of time nightfall starts the new day: "And there was evening and there was morning, the first day" (Genesis 1:5). Friday evening begins the Sabbath day for the observant Jew. There is both a human and a theological point here. The human point is that sleep comes first. We *begin* our day with rest. It is the foundation upon which a productive life stands. The theological point is that solitude constitutes the first movement of the spiritual life. Nouwen often made the point that there are three movements to the spiritual life: first solitude, then community, and then service—based upon Jesus' own practice (Luke 6:12-19). First, Jesus went up on the mountain to pray (Luke 6:12); second, he formed a community of followers (Luke 6:13-16); finally, he entered society to serve others (Luke 6:17-19). All three of these stages or movements should appear in the life of the disciple, in this order. (To place service before rest is to violate the order of creation.) While nearly everyone appreciates the need to serve, many do not understand that the first two movements (solitude and community) actually empower service. American culture tends to inspire a 24/7 kind of life. *Going* and *doing* are exalted as everything; resting and community-building are little emphasized.

How different this understanding is from Scripture. From the beginning rest is a feature of the Creator Himself: "God rested" (Gen 2:2). The Hebrew verb rendered "rest" in our English Bibles is *shabat*. God not only engaged in Sabbath rest, but he was renewed by his rest, according to Exodus 31:17, "On the seventh day God rested, and was refreshed," or, as one translation records it, "on the seventh day he rested and drew breath" (Jerusalem Bible). If God needs to catch his breath once a week, if rest and refreshment are essential to the *divine* life, what about *human* life? It is understandable why many citizens, including some Christians, rebelled against the joyless "blue laws" that once ruled over Sunday life in the United States, which infringed on what one could buy, where one could go, and what one's entertainment choices might be. However, we may have corrected one error (abolishing a prescriptive Sabbath) only to replace it with a worse one (imposing on ourselves a life of exhaustion). Rest is not a burden, but a life-giving gift and joyous freedom.

BEATITUDE FOR OUR TIME NO. 3: "HAPPY ARE THE PLAYFUL, FOR THEY WILL BE SERIOUS ACHIEVERS."

God made us playful creatures, and it is proper and honorable to exercise this prized gift, even in our adult lives. Perhaps we should occasionally pray: "Lord, remind us to play." As the historian Johan Huizinga explained, we are *homo ludens*, that is, "playful humans"—creatures of play by our very nature. Just as surely as God calls us to work, he also calls us to creative leisure. (Was it children's innocent playfulness that prompted Jesus to advise adults to become like children?) Sadly, we live in a time when children's playfulness has been scrutinized and reined in by some anxious parents and overly zealous education experts. Jonathan Kozol, author of *Death at an Early Age* and *Amazing Grace: The Lives of Children and the Conscience of a Nation*, reports a dreadful transformation in early childhood education. Some two-year-olds now have coaches who prep them for interviews to ensure their entrance into Manhattan's elite kindergartens, the "Little Ivies." Some schools become "drill and grill academies" which have little room for playfulness, silliness, and recreation, because test performance is the only consideration. In this dreary, mechanistic system the innate joy of learning is drummed out of the children, and they become as miserably routinized as their parents.

Yet play "is the serious business of child life....It is not trivial to the child or the youth...play is not only a possible, but an inevitable, factor in the formation of character."[11] And, very importantly, it lasts throughout life. It does not magically end at adolescence. Part of our weariness results not from the weight of our work but from the dreary joylessness of our working lives. We should respect leisure as an intrinsic good. Perhaps we could then say: "Blessed are those who do useless things, for they will be fulfilled." Josef Pieper argues that leisure is not just a "break" from one's work, a utilitarian pause to make us more efficient. Rather,

[l]eisure is an altogether different matter; it is no longer on the same plane;

it runs at right angles to work—just as it could be said that intuition is not the prolongation or continuation, as it were, of the work of reason, but cuts right across it, vertically. And therefore leisure does not exist for the sake of work—however much strength it may give a person to work; the point of leisure is not to be a restorative, a pick-me-up, whether mental or physical; and though it gives new strength, mentally and physically, and spiritually too, that is not the point. Leisure, like contemplation, is of a higher order than the *via activa*....No one who looks to leisure simply to restore working powers will ever discover the fruit of leisure; that person will never know the quickening that follows, as though from some deep sleep.[12]

The work ethic needs to be balanced by the "play ethic." To be fully human, we must accept the rest and refreshment that Jesus offers. Indeed, our willingness to rest is a sign of faithfulness: "He makes me lie down in green pastures; he leads me beside the still waters; he restores my soul" (Psalm 23:2-3). "Come to me, all you that are weary and are carrying heavy burdens, and I will give you rest" (Matthew 11:28). In the next chapter, we shall consider additional ways the Master brings rest to the pilgrim heart.

6

RESTING: MORE SABBATH BLESSINGS

Drop thy still dews of quietness,
Till all our strivings cease;
Take from our souls the strain and stress,
And let our ordered lives confess
The beauty of Thy peace.
—John Greenleaf Whittier

Be attentive about your time. Man will not be able to excuse himself
at the last judgment, saying to God, "You overwhelmed me with the future
when I was only capable of living in the present."
The Cloud of Unknowing

Between 1968 and 1988, the average American worker added 168 hours of work to his or her annual work load—an extra month of work each year.[1] Americans, perhaps more than any people on the earth, receive their significance from work, yet work can take us only so far. Work is a blessing, but the Book of Ecclesiastes also reminds us it is a vexation and a striving after the wind (2:23, 4:4). The great gift of a Sabbath understanding of life is that it can deliver us from the imprisonment of "salvation by work."

BEATITUDE FOR OUR TIMES NO. 4:
"HAPPY ARE THE IMPERFECTIONISTS, FOR THEY WILL ACHIEVE MUCH."

Excellence is a worthy ideal, the secret to the success of many high achievers; but the incessant pursuit of excellence also has a dark side, which is seldom talked about. Sometimes "excellence" is not about high standards. It's about neuroses. Steven Sample, President of the University of Southern California, tells the story of his own excessive perfectionism in junior high school. The demands he placed on himself were so high that he could never get his work done. One day a teacher pulled him aside and said:

> Steve, you are by nature a perfectionist; you never know when to stop trying
> to make a thing better. So here's something for you to keep in mind:
> Anything worth doing at all is worth doing poorly. It may be worth more if
> it's done well, but it's worth something if it's done poorly.[2]

This bit of counterintuitive advice helped Sample succeed in school. Today, he is recognized as one of America's most successful university presidents. He certainly believes in "excellence," yet he has achieved a great deal by learning this important truth: not every task demands perfection. Indeed, a preoccupation with excellence in every detail can paralyze a person and lead to failure.

The point is not to endorse uncaring or sloppy work, but to call us to be strategic with our limited resources. On a typical day, I receive a large number of important emails that I cannot ignore. If I were to write the perfect reply to each one of them, I would never finish my work. Furthermore, if I were to write fifty "perfect" email replies on a given day, this would mean that other more important matters would be neglected. So, I have learned to write the "just-good-enough" email reply most days. I have discovered that some things just don't deserve a lot of time, and email is one of them.

Sample points out that when General Patton was moving swiftly towards Berlin near the end of World War II, his troops had to stop to build bridges over rivers, but Patton didn't want his men to build the world's best bridge. He wanted bridges that were just good enough for his tanks and troops to cross the river only once in the direction of Berlin. To do otherwise would have been a dangerous waste of time and resources. History is filled with the tragic stories of those who invested all their time in lesser things, only to neglect the greater things. Getting one's priorities right and letting lesser matters go is spiritual wisdom.

A theological truth resides in the beatitude of "Happy are the imperfectionists." It is a roundabout way of saying, "Blessed are humble sinners, for they know that their perfection is found in their Savior, not in themselves." Our righteousness, our peace of mind, and our perfection come from without (our Savior), not from within (ourselves). Even as we strive for excellence, we remember that we live by the graciousness of the Perfect One, not by our own strength, wisdom, cleverness, or achievement.

BEATITUDE FOR OUR TIMES NO. 5: "HAPPY ARE THOSE WHO DRIVE IN THE SLOW LANE, FOR THEY WILL ARRIVE IN PEACE (OR IN ONE PIECE)."

I often must negotiate the busy freeways of Los Angeles. Some days it's pretty harrowing. On the really bad days, I've found that it is better to arrive a few minutes late in order to be less frazzled and frantic. To reinforce this behavior, I've joined a movement that has brought me some peace. It's the "slowing movement." For example, on the freeways, I sometimes deliberately choose a slow lane and stay with it. In the supermarket or the pharmacy I cultivate patience by deliberately choosing to place myself in positions where I have to wait.[3] It has also given me the opportunity to start to learn the radical practice of "guerrilla compassion," by saying a prayer of blessing over each person ahead of me in my line or in the next line at the check-out counter.[4]

Especially for those who seem particularly hurried, worried, or rude, I try to imagine their hidden struggles, crises, and worries; and I silently bless them. I've almost entirely abandoned drive-through windows at banks and fast-food restaurants. First, I've noticed that the service inside is often better than the outside service. Second, going inside provides me a little physical exercise, which I always need. Third, I enjoy the face-to-face contact with the clerk behind the counter. "Slowing" is good for us.

BEATITUDE FOR OUR TIMES NO. 6:
"BLESSED ARE THOSE WHO BUILD WALLS FOR THEY WILL BE FULLY CONNECTED."

Walls have gotten a bad rap lately. The mantras of our day celebrate seamlessness. Walls have come to signify something negative—exclusivity, isolation, and division. "Something there is that doesn't love a wall," Robert Frost writes. Jesus often broke down the walls of his own day. As we shall see in Chapter 7, Jesus is the supreme "boundary-crosser." But the One who challenges settled frontiers also invites us to maintain a few walls. In fact, some boundaries do make better neighbors. It is important to distinguish between good and bad walls.

Biology, politics, Scripture, and human experience teach us in various ways that some walls are essential for health, for walls not only divide but also protect and shelter. A house without walls is no house at all. In biology cells can do their work because they have healthy walls or membranes. These boundaries preserve the homeostasis which makes biological processes, and hence life, possible. If the walls or membranes dissolve, the organism dies. To be without boundaries is to be vulnerable to pathology and death.

In the realm of religion, spiritual maturity and holiness are possible only if there are certain kinds of separation. Saints by definition are those who are "bordered off" from things that compromise or contaminate. "Paul, an apostle, [is] *set apart* for the gospel of God" (Romans 1:1, my emphasis). "Therefore come out from them, and be separate from them, says the Lord, and touch nothing unclean; then I will welcome you, and I will be your father, and you will be my sons and daughters, says the Lord Almighty" (2 Corinthians 6:17-18).

When our boundaries are porous and dilapidated, we fall into crisis. For example, families today struggle because certain walls have fallen. Mary Pipher writes:

> For the first time in two thousand years of Western civilization, families live in houses without walls. That is, they live in a world in which walls offer no protection. Technology has brought the outside world into the living room. Social scientists have walked in and second-guessed the way

parents function. Crime on the nightly news makes all places feel dangerous. Electronic media seeps into the interstices of homes and teaches children ways of thinking, feeling and behaving that are at odds with common sense. Families are reeling under the pressures of a culture they can't control.[5]

Just as a house cannot stand without walls, neither can a home. We are in trouble because we have divided where God has joined together, and we have joined together where God has called for separation. The evidence of this loss may be seen in our easy rejection of Sabbath rest, and our loss of the sense of the sacred, which means the abandonment of anything "set apart"—sacred space, sacred time, family mealtimes, or any special time without phone, email, iPods, PDAs, and so forth. "Multi-tasking" may be a virtue in certain limited settings, but it is disastrous as a way of life because it means that no one thing ever receives our total devotion. If all the world becomes "the world of work," then we have rendered impossible any encounter with the holy (which, by definition, requires devoted attention). Once work and leisure become homogenized, we fail to do our jobs well (for we are never fully rested); and we fail to rest once our work stops (for our work haunts us). No wonder so many of us are anxious, weary insomniacs.

BEATITUDE FOR OUR TIMES NO. 7:
"HAPPY ARE THOSE WHO SAY 'NO,' FOR THEY WILL BE AFFIRMED."

In *The Freedom of Simplicity* Richard Foster tells the story of his ironic dilemma. The man best known for promoting the spiritual disciplines in our time became so busy traveling the country talking about spirituality that he faced exhaustion. One day in a Washington, D.C., airport, while reading Thomas Kelley's *A Testament of Devotion*, his eyes fell upon these words: "We have seen and known some people who seem to have found this deep Center of living, where the fretful calls of life are integrated, where No as well as Yes can be said with confidence." Kelly's invitation to find holiness in the "no" as well as in the "yes" provoked a life-changing epiphany in Foster, who had understood the obligation to accept every call to serve, but who had not comprehended the spiritual necessity of sometimes saying no. Foster writes:

> Alone, I sat in the airport watching the rain splatter against the window.
> Tears fell on my coat. It was a holy place, an altar, the chair where I sat. I
> was never to be the same. Quietly, I asked God to give me the ability to say
> No when it was right and good.[6]

That moment proved to be a turning point in Richard Foster's life and ministry. He decided to dedicate Friday nights to his family and limit his speaking engagements. He turned the corner and found that by saying no on certain occasions, he was empowered to serve God and others even more effectively.

Many people say yes indiscriminately—even when the net effect is bad. Of course, there are times when Christians must say yes even though it is personally costly. That is the nature of the sacrifice to which we are called. In the midst of the tsunamis of life, one cannot enjoy the luxury of retreat from the fray. To walk away in a crisis is dereliction of duty. Still, not everything that calls to us is a crisis. Jesus models the point well. Consider that Jesus lived approximately thirty-three years, yet he spent about thirty of those years, roughly 90% of his earthly life, out of the limelight, in quiet, in preparation, away from any form of public ministry. Efficiency experts examining Jesus' "productivity" might conclude that he was a slacker. Consider the experts' logic: How much more healing and teaching Jesus might have done had he started younger and worked harder. Consider further that during his brief ministry he enjoyed a fair amount of "down time," Sabbath rests, and retreats—even when the crowds clamored for attention. How many more people could Jesus have taught and healed had he merely cut out his retreats to Mary, Martha, and Lazarus's house or his prayer time on the Mount of Olives? Dubious as this kind of argument may seem, many of us try to be busier than the Master.

It takes careful discernment to determine when to say no. Some possible reasons to say no include these: (1) When yes is really about building one's material wealth or enhancing one's ego, rather than advancing a good or essential cause; in other words when yes is about me; (2) when yes hurts those you love; (3) when one's yes is prompted by an automatic, uncritical response, rather than the product of self-examination, prayer, and discernment; (4) when one finds oneself growing weaker and weaker, spiritually speaking, the more one does; (5) when one finds oneself fulfilling a lower good, while sacrificing a higher one; (6) and when one finds, at the end of the day, one is becoming someone he or she doesn't even like.

BEATITUDE FOR OUR TIMES NO. 8: "BLESSED ARE THOSE WHO KNOW THE TIE THAT BINDS, FOR THEY WILL KNOW THE FREEDOM OF BELONGING."

Just as the right kind of separation can renew our spirits and bodies, so also connecting with others in the right way can banish exhaustion and revive our spirits. Consider assessing what happens emotionally and physically when we spend time with others. If you are like me, some people give you energy, while others deplete you. I try to monitor my spirit and take note of those who buoy me and those who do not. I have learned that I can endure a fair amount of tension, conflict, and even mountains of labor, provided I am connected to others in the right way. I am energized and empowered, in other words, by community. I wonder if this was part of the secret of Jesus' ministry. He had his twelve, his three, and his one best friend.

One of my favorite moments in Mitch Albom's bestselling memoir *Tuesdays with Morrie* occurs when the dying teacher, Morrie, reminds Mitch that we need others when we are born—for no one gives birth to himself or rears himself. We need others in our last frail years too, Morrie says. But the real "secret" of life, Morrie tells Mitch, is that we also need each other in the in-between years as well. The tie that binds, the sweet fellowship of loving and caring brothers and sisters in the faith, is not constricting at all but liberating. Time spent in authentic community is also a kind of Sabbath rest.

Lady Julian once wrote, "God did not say, 'You shall not be tempest-tossed, you shall not be work-weary, you shall not be discomforted.' But he said, 'you shall not be overcome.'"[7] Jesus promised that his yoke would be easy and his burden light (Matthew 11:30). The balanced life is not always the care-free or the retired life, though I recommend taking it easy occasionally, removing oneself from the noise of the marketplace and relishing an uncommon idleness now and then. The homely proverb is wise counsel: "Stop often and set frequent." More often than not, though, we must find our measures of solitude and Sabbath even within the maelstrom, not only after it passes.

We find peace, then, not through escape, but by paying attention to the shifts, the alternations, and the movements of the whole life. Wholeness comes to us by way of paradox: there is a time to disappear and a time to be present; a time to retreat and a time to advance; a time to withdraw and a time to engage. Our greatest problem may not be the crushing loads of work which our jobs and guilty consciences dump on us, but our flat refusal to invoke boundaries and protect our sacred spaces, our refusal to lie down in the green pastures to which our Shepherd wishes to lead us.

The Internet illustrates the problem perfectly. This astonishing means of connection allows us to stay in touch with friends, family, and fellow workers around the world; yet this same tool can morph into a kind of prison, profoundly isolating us from people who are near at hand. How many people obsess over their computers, effectively shutting themselves off from essential contact with friends and family who may be across the room or down the hall?

Many people in traditional, less advanced cultures know hard work—long hours and back-breaking labor. Burdensome toil is not new to the human condition, but what may be relatively new is the radical erasure of sacred spaces and sacred times. I speak of the destruction of the psychological and spiritual respites that make renewal possible. A 24/7 culture is deeply hostile to the human spirit. People of faith must acknowledge, critique, and resist those forces that make rest impossible. Sadly, some of these negative forces actually emanate from religious institutions. Too many people attend churches that fill the weekend with endless activities, making a mockery of any notion of Sabbath rest.

The solution is not a return to some ideal or romantic past when we did it right; but to create appropriate, balanced means of quiet and connection, and to join other believers in a covenanted commitment to protect sacred times.

Rabbi Levi saw a man running in the street, and asked him, "Why do you run?" He replied, "I am running after my good fortune!" Rabbi Levi tells him, "Silly man, your good fortune has been trying to chase you, but you are running too fast."[8]

People are desperate for the good fortune of spiritual wholeness and peace of mind. They spin their wheels ever faster, and their goals recede as the velocity mounts. If they stopped and became quiet, they might find just what they are seeking. Having been created in the divine image, every pilgrim heart shares the same essential need of *shabat*. Answering Jesus' quiet invitation is the place to begin: *"Come away to a deserted place all by yourselves and rest awhile"* (Mark 6:31). If we hear and obey, we will be blessed indeed.

7

BEFRIENDING: THE MUTUAL REGARD AND CARE OF SOULS

No one has greater love than this, to lay down one's life for one's friends...
I do not call you servants any longer..., but I have called you friends.
John 15:13-15

A man of many companions may come to ruin,
but there is a friend who sticks closer than a brother.
Proverbs 18:24 (NIV)

Those friends thou hast, and their adoption tried,
Grapple them unto thy soul with hoops of steel.
—Shakespeare

A friend of mine, a minister, once told his father about an exciting new mentoring program which was being introduced in the minister's congregation. After listening to the son's enthusiastic description of the new effort, the father replied drolly, "We used to have a program like that in my church when I was growing up. We called them 'friends.'" I am glad that churches, schools, and other organizations have initiated mentoring programs; but could it be that the popularity of formal mentoring initiatives is a sign that our culture has forgotten how to foster friendships naturally? Is friendship a lost art? Many think so.

There once was a flourishing literature on friendship, composed by some of the world's greatest thinkers—Aristotle, Plutarch, Cicero, Augustine, Montaigne, for example. The Greeks had their stories of Damon and Pythias (or Phintias). In one version Pythias was sentenced to death for plotting against King Dionysius of Syracuse. Damon offered himself in the place of his friend. Upon seeing such extraordinary loyalty and love, the king forgave Pythias and then asked to be admitted to their circle of friendship. It was virtually commonplace in the ancient world to write, as Horace did, "Whilst I am in my right mind, there is nothing I will compare with a delightful friend."[1] Similarly, the Jews celebrated the friendship of Jonathan and David (1 Samuel 18-20): "Jonathan made David swear again by his love for him, for he loved him as he loved his own life" (20:17).

The literature of early Christianity emphasizes the importance of friendship. The Gospel of John honors Jesus' friendship with "the disciple whom Jesus loved," commonly thought to be John himself.[2] Augustine's *Confessions* contains the stories of devoted friends like Alypius, whom Augustine dubs his "heart's brother."[3] Augustine gives particular attention to an unnamed friend who died young, whom the writer calls "half my soul." Quoting the poet Ovid, Augustine confesses that "my soul and his soul were 'one soul in two bodies.'"[4]

Friendship remains a familiar theme throughout the Middle Ages and the Renaissance. The twelfth-century English monk Aelred (or Ethelred) of Rievaulx wrote the classic treatise, *Spiritual Friendship*, and one of Montaigne's most famous essays is devoted to the subject.[5] Many of Shakespeare's plays, both comedies and tragedies, reflect a preoccupation with the nature of friendship—its beauty, its value, its challenges. In recent years, the spiritual meaning of friendship has been revived, largely through the rediscovery of the devotional classics and the traditions of spiritual direction, but most people are generally unfamiliar with the practices of earlier Christianity.[6]

THE LOST ART?

Friendship as a serious subject (and some would say as a serious practice) fell into neglect in modern times. C. S. Lewis lamented the decline in his classic *The Four Loves*: "To the Ancients, Friendship seemed the happiest and most fully human of all loves; the crown of life and the school of virtue. The modern world, in comparison, ignores it."[7] Many would argue that mature friendship is rare, especially among contemporary American men. A professor of sociology once told me as much, when she concluded, after studying friendships at length, that American men are generally good at "side-by-side" relationships: they can bowl side by side, watch sporting events side by side, hunt or fish side-by-side; but what they cannot do is face one another and engage in a deep, heart-felt conversation. Thomas S. Fortson, Jr., president and chief executive of the evangelical ministry Promise Keepers, asserts that the first characteristic of American men is that they are friendless.[8]

The contrast with previous generations is more than considerable, and one must ask if there are consequences to the decline of interest in spiritual friendship. The short answer is yes, because authentic spirituality is corporate by nature. God always intended the pilgrim heart to travel in company. Without partners for the journey, we are ever in peril. Many believers are chronically lonely in their spiritual search. Emotionally detached, without faithful companions to hold them accountable, they are particularly vulnerable to temptation.

Some years ago I became interested in men in crisis. Some were depressed. Others were tempted by affairs or close to abandoning their religious or family commitments. As I befriended these men, I noticed something striking. While their surface stories were considerably different, I noticed that the "deep structures" of their circumstances were often similar. In particular I noticed that they were alienated, disengaged, or emotionally isolated. Why was this? No doubt the forces creating their various situations were complex, but it was pretty clear that the culture's emphasis upon radical individualism was part of the problem.

America's seminal heroes, from Ben Franklin to Ralph Waldo Emerson, preached a persuasive gospel of autonomy and self-reliance. Popular culture tells us in countless ways to stand alone, to be independent, and not to tell the truths of our inner beings to anyone. The message has sunk deep into the hearts and minds of millions; and many—men and women alike—feel compelled to go it alone, to invent their own "spirituality," in effect, to save themselves.

The trouble is, we were never created to live isolated lives, and to try to do so is to invite crushing loneliness and personal disaster. A rich spiritual life presupposes a rich communal life, and a communal life presupposes rich friendships. "I have called you friends," the Master Teacher said. For Jesus discipleship *is* friendship:

> No one has greater love than this, to lay down one's life for one's friends. You are my friends if you do what I command you. I do not call you servants any longer, because the servant does not know what the master is doing; but I have called you friends, because I have made known to you everything that I have heard from my father. (John 15:13-15)

Just as Abraham was the friend of God, all who follow in Abraham's footsteps have also been called to be friends of God and friends to one another. In fact, a happy outcome to being a friend of God is the invitation to join a vast community of friends.

THREE KINDS OF FRIENDSHIP

Scripture presents friendship under multiple aspects or dimensions. The first level of friendship is universal in nature—the love for all humanity. Because "God so loved the world," we too practice a general charity for all God's creatures, extending peace and goodwill to all people, all races, genders, and classes. It is a friendship so broad that it can even include our enemies. Second, there is a special love for those who follow Jesus: "Love the family of believers," Peter writes in his first letter (2:17). This special affection for the community of faith is expressed in John Fawcett's classic hymn:

> Blest be the tie that binds
>
> Our hearts in Christian love;
>
> The fellowship of kindred minds
>
> Is like to that above.

But there is a third kind of friendship which entails a partner in faith, a "soul-friend," one who mentors us and holds us accountable in special ways. It is this third form of friendship that seems to be especially rare in our time. I know dedicated servants of God, some of them ministers, who do not have a single close friend with whom they share their spiritual struggles. It is as though a great tradition, at least two thousand years old, has been lost to us.

Spiritual friendship is often described in the literature of the monastics. Celtic

Christianity stressed the importance of acquiring an *anamchara* (Gaelic for "soul-friend"). Esther de Waal writes:

> Here is the truest and deepest form of friendship...that opening of one's heart to another which leads to *hesychia* [rest], serenity and peace of heart. The importance of everyone, cleric and lay, male and female, having a soul-friend, is a tacit acknowledgment of the role of a spiritual mentor and of the deep human need for the experience of reconciliation and healing.[9]

There is a familiar story of St. Brigit, who once engaged her foster son in a conversation at dinner. She inquired whether he had a soul-friend. He replied that he had had such a friend, but that he was now dead,

> and from that moment [St. Brigit] watched the young man's food being put directly into the trunk of his body since he was now without a head. "Go forth and eat nothing until you get a soul-friend, for anyone without a soul-friend is like a body without a head; is like the water of a polluted lake, neither good for drinking nor for washing. That is the person without a soul-friend."[10]

According to de Waal, soul-friendships were common in medieval Ireland. They existed "between men and women, women and women, men and men, cleric and lay. The soul-friend was the spiritual guide who helped everyone to find his or her own path....It was true friendship, with warmth and intimacy and honesty, and there is a profound respect for the other's wisdom, despite age or gender differences, as the source of blessing."[11]

The failure to make healthy spiritual friendships a central mission of the church is costly. Years ago, when Carley Dodd, David Lewis, and I conducted research into the spiritual lives of adolescents, we discovered that their behavior and attitudes were closely related to the quality of their friendships.[12] As every parent soon learns, their children's friends are a remarkably accurate indicator of what is going on in the life and heart of their child. The secret, though, is that there is a corresponding insight to be found in the adult's life too. Our relationships—or our lack of them—is a telling fact.

THE MARKS OF THE SOUL-FRIEND

My own life has involved quite a long quest for mature and lasting relationships. Though I have experienced periods of disappointment and loneliness, especially after moving to a new place to live or work, I have been blessed by friends in Jesus who offer spiritual care. Peter says that other human beings can love us with the love of God, so that they become bearers of grace to us (1 Peter 4:8-10). In my experience, such brotherly kindness not only "covers a multitude of sins" (1 Peter 4:8), but it encourages me and empowers me to live for God.

Through the years I have found certain recurring hallmarks of mature, spiritual friendship. First is *protection* and *safety*. In his novel *Good as Gold* Joseph Heller includes a conversation between two men in government service, Bruce Gold and Ralph. Though they have known each other since college days, the issue arises as to whether or not they are truly friends. Bruce probes to find out whether Ralph is a real friend:

> "I suppose you're right, Ralph. The important thing is not our social worlds but our friendship. There's a definition of a friend I once heard expressed by my Swedish publisher. He's Jewish, Ralph, and he lived in Germany under Hitler as a child until his family escaped. He has only one test of a friend now, he told me. 'Would he hide me?' is the question he asks. It's pretty much my test of a friend too, when I come down to it. Ralph, if Hitler returns, would you hide me?"
>
> The question threw Ralph into a flurry and he clambered to his feet, his fair skin turning pink. "Oh, gosh, Bruce," he exclaimed hastily, "we're not friends...."
>
> Gold felt this more than he wished to show. "You used my work at school, Ralph. We were pretty close then."
>
> "That was college, Bruce," said Ralph, "and it was important that I get my degree. But this is only government. People in government don't have friends, Bruce, just interests and ambitions."[13]

At the core of friendship is safety, whether physical or spiritual. Friendships save lives, as one sees in the story of David and Jonathan (1 Samuel 19:1-3). David's survival depended upon Jonathan's reporting to him, "My father Saul is trying to kill you; therefore be on guard tomorrow morning; stay in a secret place and hide yourself" (1 Samuel 19:2). Just as two G.I. buddies in a foxhole can watch each other's backs, so Ecclesiastes says:

> Two are better than one, because they have a good reward for their toil. For if they fall, one will lift up the other; but woe to one who is alone and falls and does not have another to help....And though one might prevail against another, two will withstand one. A threefold cord is not easily broken. (Ecclesiastes 4:9-12)

In Martin Marty's words, "We have friends, or we are friends, in order that we do not get killed."[14]

Within the question "Who will hide me?" lurks the darker question, "Would you betray me?" Betrayal (think of Judas) often annihilates friendship, and its milder cousin "abandonment" works its destructive work as well. There are fewer more plaintive words than Jesus' query to his few remaining followers: "Do you also wish to go away?" A "fair-weather friend" is an oxymoron. "A friend loves at all times" (Proverbs 17:17). Yet there is grace when we fail. Peter and the other disciples' betrayal of Jesus did not end the friendship. Confession and forgiveness provide a way back when a friendship is ruptured. Nevertheless, fidelity is an essential and expected feature of friendship. Jonathan's trust in David's absolute reliability (which perfectly mirrors David's trust in Jonathan) speaks loudly about the ancient world's conviction that real friendship provides security: "I know that as long as I live you will show me faithful friendship" (1 Samuel 20:14, Revised English Bible).

Loyalty, however, is not enough. After all, there is a kind of honor even among thieves, gangsters, and cranks, who cheerfully protect their confederates for unholy purposes. Spiritual friendship is not about utility or *quid pro quo* benefits. Much more is required, in particular, the virtues of love, temperance, and moral accountability. Soul-friends most certainly tell the truth, even when it is painful—about themselves and what they see in each other, good or bad. Jesus said, "I have called you friends because I have made known to you *everything*" (John 15:15, my emphasis). When the disciples' behavior was substandard, Jesus held them accountable. He critiqued their pettiness, religious chauvinism, rivalry, pride, and faithlessness. Yet he loved them through and through.

My best friends are those who tell me the truth with patience and compassion. They invite me to share my struggles, doubts, and sins. When I am wavering, I know whom I can call. Three questions help me distinguish my garden variety relationships from my soul-friends. The first question is Joseph Heller's "Who will hide me?" which is to ask, "Am I safe with you?" Second, I ask, "Could I call you at 2:00 a.m. if I were in need?" Fortunately, this is not a test I have often performed, but knowing that I have friends who will be there for me is a great comfort. The third question is this: "Can I tell you who I am?" or "Can I tell you my story?"

We all need someone to carry our sorrows, our doubts, our questions. This means we need someone who is slow to judge us or fix us. We need someone who patiently listens, holds our shadows in trust, carries us when necessary, and inspires us to do better. We need someone to whom we can tell the truth about our lives, no matter how stained, flawed, or complicated we are: "[C]onfess your sins to one another, and pray for one another, so that you may be healed" (James 5:16). If confession and mutual intercessory prayer bring healing, then the reverse may well be true. In the refusal to live in truth with others, unnecessary illness and pain may be our lot.

Soul-friendships are rare today because they are costly. Most of all they require our time, as they are only sustainable with frequent contact. Friendships on auto-pilot waste away. Vital and healthy relationships, however, undergo periodic renewal, as one sees in the example of Jonathan and David: "Jonathan pledged himself *afresh* to David because of his love for him" (1 Samuel 20:17, Revised English Bible, my emphasis). I have been able to sustain friends for twenty and thirty years only through a lot of effort—letters, calls, email, and regular personal contact. Even though some of my best friends live in different parts of the country and we have been separated for years, the friendship continues to flourish because we have agreed to communicate regularly and spend time together. We write, we travel together, and we retreat together.

Of course, this takes a considerable investment of time. William Shakespeare suggested one of the fundamental ingredients of a friendship: real friends are those who "do converse and waste the time together."[15] I've never seen a long-lasting friendship that did not entail "wasting time" together; but with a career to build, a mortgage to pay, and a family to raise, who has time for this luxury? One woman once told me that her husband used to have close friends, but he hadn't developed any new ones since his college days (twenty years before) because he just had "no time." My reply is this: *we have time for what we value.*

Spiritual friendship also requires something else—*distance.* This may seem paradoxical, since friendship implies closeness, but mature friendships flourish when the friends respect distance. Friendship is not enmeshment. The friend offers a listening ear, an understanding heart, and a helping hand. But he or she also offers space for one to be. Augustine tells the wrenching story of a great mistake he made in a friendship in his youth. He and his unnamed friend were the same age and shared "identical interests," and so their friendship looked like a good one. But Augustine—needy, precocious, and assertive—pressured his friend to abandon his faith and turn to superstition and mythology. "We were deeply dependent upon one another," Augustine writes. When the friend became ill and died, Augustine was overwhelmed with grief, anger, and depression: "I boiled with anger, sighed, wept, and was at my wits' end....I carried my lacerated and bloody soul when it was unwilling to be carried by me. I found no place where I could put it down.... Everything was an object of horror, even light itself."[16] Later, as a mature Christian, Augustine reflected on his unhealthy devotion to his friend. Augustine confessed his mistake: "I had poured out my soul on to the sand by loving a person sure to die as if he would never die." He had transferred his love for the Creator to one of God's creatures; he had loved a friend as a substitute for God; he had also failed to respect fully the personhood of his friend.

Though friendships remained a central concern all of his life, the author of the *Confessions* learned not to substitute friendship for God. A friend is not a means to a selfish purpose, an "egotism *à deux*," to borrow Erich Fromm's phrase.[17] In the words of the poet Rilke, "two solitudes protect and touch and greet each other."[18] Martin Marty warns against friendships that do not respect the uniqueness and inviolability of the friend: "The impulse to refashion and duplicate one's self in another is a burden friendship cannot bear or outlast. Otherness is the key to friendship....'Using' friends is the death of friendship."[19] Thus there can be no lasting friendship where there is coercion or inequality.[20] It is striking that Jesus never twists the arms of his beloved disciples to make them "do the right thing." Friendship flies under the flag of freedom.

The ancient philosophers developed a sophisticated understanding of friendship, but it was Jesus who most fully articulated the spiritual dimension to friendship. For Jesus, friendship is a particular blessing that comes with life in the kingdom of God. Because the friend is a partaker, a bearer, of the divine nature (1 Peter 1:4), and he or she is destined for eternity, the relationship is sacred. A friend is, therefore, a potential channel of grace and a mirror of divine love. For this reason, Martin Marty suggests, we not only sing "What a friend we have in Jesus," but we say "What a Jesus we have in a friend."[21]

Mature friendship is rich in *compassion* and *self-sacrifice*: "No one has greater love than this, to lay down one's life for one's friends" (John 15:13). The theme was well observed by the beloved disciple John, who declared: "We know love by this, that he laid down his life for us—and we ought to lay down our lives for one another" (1 John 3:16). According to Aelred, if God is love, then it follows that "God is friendship" too.[22]

Spiritual friendships are characterized by empathy, compassion, and careful attention to the other. One of the wonders of friends is their ability to express solidarity with us:

> Were I elect like you,
> I would encircle me with love, and raise
> A rampart of my fellows; it should seem
> Impossible for me to fail, so watched
> By gentle friends who made my cause their own.[23]

"[S]o watched / By gentle friends who made my cause their own...." How apt is Robert Browning's description of the calling of the soul-friend!

During certain periods of my life I have been discouraged or uncertain of my direction. On occasions too numerous to count, a friend appeared at my door or sent an encouraging message, timely interventions that offered me good counsel or encouragement. Many friendships may have been born out of happy circumstances; but it can often be a crisis that becomes the strong bridge to another person, initiating a friendship that withstands the tempests of life. Stuart Miller writes:

> In some complicated way, friendship at its most perfect is related to deep suffering and deep illness; the acute horror of being forced into desolation by a society that clearly has little real interest in human values. So when people go toward each other and love one another, there's a deep medication. Real friendship, then, is a kind of divine act that enables two people to share feelings, to have feelings that life denies continually.[24]

Once, in a time of distress, I wrote this to a trusted friend:

> If I'm an authority on anything, it may be friendship. Not because I'm the perfect practitioner of it, but because I am the perfect recipient of friendship upon friendship—grace upon grace. Most often I've known the rich depths of spiritual friendship in moments of personal crisis when I felt abandoned, in despair, or overwhelmed. It was Christ in the other, modeling divine love, loyalty, and presence, that has saved my soul more than once. It's come through unexpected phone calls and impromptu visits at my door and through countless cards and notes over the years. Often the words have been amazingly simple and brief. I remember, for example, a time when I felt very alienated from everyone around me. In my aloneness, I said to my friend, "Sometimes I feel like I belong on a different planet from everyone else." And my friend said, "Whatever planet you end up on, I want to be on it with you." How simple! The words, though, were healing. On countless occasions since, when I've felt myself slipping into old feelings of alienation, I just recall those words, "I want to be on that planet with you" and everything is almost automatically better. The loneliness diminishes. Hope revives.

There are pilgrim hearts like these in the world, embodiments of grace; and it is our joyous duty and our everlasting privilege to seek them out and hold them fast.

Yet we cannot accumulate friends like so many trophies. Friends are not objects to be found and collected. Our calling isn't so much to find friends as to become friends to others. I am not even sure it is possible to "find" friends. Instead, we befriend others, and in the befriending, worthy companions are mysteriously born. As imitators of Jesus we are here to grant to others the gifts of safety, attentiveness, compassion, empathy, accountability, truth-telling, loyalty, distance, time, forgiveness, spiritual care, and selfless love. In offering such graces to others, friendships emerge.

TAKING OFF THE MASKS

The pilgrim heart is not content merely to receive grace from others. The heart shaped by God extends grace, selflessly and lavishly. Those who follow Jesus in earnest accept the risk that all relationships entail, knowing that love tendered to others does not always return in kind. "Do good, and lend, expecting nothing in return" (Luke 6:35) is a principle for friendship building as much as advice on how to dole out one's possessions. Those who seek mature relationships invest themselves heavily in the hard task of finding others, looking them in the eye, listening to their hearts, and resisting judgment. It may take years to develop such relationships, but they are worth the effort. Our own hearts depend upon this effort, and so does the survival of community.

Lewis Mumford, the great architectural critic and historian, and Henry A. Murray, the famed psychologist, were very different men who formed a lasting friendship. A considerable correspondence developed between them over a period of forty years beginning in 1929. Near the beginning of their friendship, Mumford wrote Murray: "Falling in friendship is a rarer thing, I think, than falling in love; and while I have a handful of partial friendships, I have yet to experience a friendship that is complete, that involves all one's attitudes and interests—with no disguises or only profile views. Heaven knows such friendships are rare; probably more so than a complete marriage." Many years later, in August of 1942, Murray describes "the delight, the wonder, the sympathy, exhilaration, pride in fellow-feeling" that continued to stir him as he corresponded with his friend. While such friendships may be rare, they are possible and even probable among those who take the way of Jesus seriously.

Friendship is not dead today, but it is in distress. The followers of Jesus must take friendship very seriously, for it has a sacramental dimension to it. Simone Weil wrote to her spiritual mentor, Father Perrin: "human relations perpetually enshrine the light of God." Friendship, she wrote, is "an intimation and a reflection of divine love."[25] Aelred, the Cistercian abbot of Rievaulx, believed that Christ indwelt relationships, so he began his classic work on spiritual friendship like this: "Here we are, you and I, and I hope a third, Christ is in our midst."[26] Every pilgrim heart, I believe, sooner or later experiences the truth to which Aelred and Weil point.

When I was a young man, it was the minister of the local congregation and an elderly lady next door who befriended me in just the right ways, offering me encouraging words, extending praise and encouragement, planting seeds of faith and dreams and possibilities that would eventually bear fruit, though in some cases it would be decades later. What if these soul-friends had not come along just when they did? It is impossible for me to imagine. In fact, it was not primarily the doctrinal instruction in the congregation of my youth that sustained me in the ensuing years, but the example, witness and care of spiritual friends. In college a few teachers and college friends patiently endured my questions and my doubts; and, in time, in a strong marriage, I found a spouse who modeled the grace of faithful friendship most completely. The presence and patience of these have made me strong when I was weak.

I like to imagine the grand surprise I will get when, in heaven, I meet all "the angels unawares" (Hebrews 13:2, Authorized Version), those divine emissaries of grace who crossed my path in times of need. Who will they be? Of course I do not know, but I suspect some of those angels incognito carry out their ministrations today under the name of "friend." It may be just as C. S. Lewis supposed: "This love, free from instinct, free from all duties but those which love has freely assumed, almost wholly free from jealousy, and free without qualification from the need to be needed, is eminently spiritual. It is the sort of love one can imagine between angels."[27]

8

CONFESSING: I SWEAR TO TELL THE *WHOLE* TRUTH

If we say we have no sin, we deceive ourselves, and the truth is not in us.
If we confess our sins, he who is faithful and just will forgive us our sins
and cleanse us from all unrighteousness.
1 John 1:8-9

In a room where people unanimously maintain a conspiracy of silence,
one word of truth sounds like a pistol shot.
—Czeslaw Milosz

Of all the chapters in this book, this one is the hardest to write, not because the concept is so deep or complex, but because it strikes so close to home. The pilgrim heart is a confessional heart, a heart that faces the truth, accepts the truth, and tells the truth—especially the truth about oneself. There are countless social forces that tempt us to soften the truth, to spin the facts, or merely to stay superficial. For one thing, we live a harsh and competitive world. The cost of truth-telling can be extraordinarily high, especially in communities of faith, where everyone is expected to look better than they are.

Ironically, the Christian community's demand for respectability often increases the dishonesty. Dietrich Bonhoeffer, in his classic *Life Together*, exposes the temptation of false piety among belivers: "The pious fellowship permits no one to be a sinner. So everybody must conceal his sin from himself and from the fellowship. We dare not be sinners. Many Christians are unthinkably horrified when a real sinner is suddenly discovered among the righteous. So we remain alone with our sin, living in lies and hypocrisy."[1]

Thus, the very assumption and expectation of our righteousness makes the confession of sin an impossibility, an intolerable burden on the follower of Jesus. Perhaps even worse, it presents an image of intolerable smugness and arrogance to outsiders, a stumbling block to those who might otherwise consider the merits of the faith. Jesus exposes such religious hypocrisy, colorfully rendered in *The Message*: "Your lives are roadblocks to God's kingdom. You refuse to enter, and won't let anyone else in either. You're hopeless, you religion scholars and Pharisees! Frauds! You go halfway around the world to make a convert, but once you get him you make him into a replica of yourselves, double-damned!" (Matthew 23:13-15).

Our inability to confess our obvious and hidden failures greatly damages our spiritual lives and our credibility. Our witness rings hollow. Our carefully packaged faith that hides faults haunts us and angers others. When things go awry, as they will, it becomes second nature to blame others rather than take responsibility. Thus, Christians can reside in communities where the truth rarely is spoken and where disappointment, bitterness, cynicism, and anger simmer for years. Finally, the day comes when the frustration explodes. Nearly everyone is surprised at the intensity of the blow-up. What happened and why?

Often the explosion is the inevitable consequence of Christians not telling the truth of their lives—their hurts over their troubled marriages, the disappointment with parents and children, their sadness and anger over harsh and unfair words spoken at church, the chronic pain of a dysfunctional relationship at work. Mark it down. A Christian who is not confessional is in peril—a danger to himself and to the community. An unconfessed Christian is an oxymoron, like a baker who hates bread or a fisherman who won't go near the water.

Two incontrovertible facts lead us to the central importance of truth-telling in the life of the disciple. Fact one: *Everyone who lives is deeply hurt by others.* Fact two: *Everyone who lives has deeply hurt others.* These two givens, abstract and general, look safe on the page. But it's quite another thing to reformulate these general truths in more personal terms: *I* have been wounded by others, and *I* have wounded others.

Yet these words, so hard to write, so hard to say, are true. And the truth is far more momentous than this. As I come to know God, a third great and painful and inescapable truth emerges: *I have wounded and offended my God, the one who loved me and brought me into being.* It is this sense of utter moral and spiritual failure that prompted Isaiah to exclaim when confronted by the holy God: "Woe is me! I am lost, for I am a man of unclean lips, and I live among a people of unclean lips; yet my eyes have seen the King, the Lord of hosts!" (Isaiah 6:5). It's the same sort of reaction one finds in Peter's audience that day in Jerusalem when he told them that they had assisted in the crucifixion of the Messiah: "Now when they heard this, they were cut to the heart and said to Peter and the other apostles, 'Brothers, what should we do?'" (Acts. 2:37). The daily drumbeat of depressing news confirms the unrelenting witness of Scripture: Human beings are hurting and hurtful beings, and a great deal of the injury is self-inflicted. As Paul puts it, we rend our common humanity, biting and devouring one another (Galatians 5:15).

Can we break the cycle of pain? Can we heal "the eternal wound of existence," as Nietzsche called it? The answer to these questions is available, I believe, only after we have listened to the Good News. (The possibility of healing is, indeed, the *good* in the Good News.) But a necessary premise of Good News is that something very bad is going on in our lives for which the Good News is the welcome remedy. If we cannot see the bad news in our lives and confess it, we block the one pathway to hope. So, an essential step is truth-telling. Telling the truth about our dilemma initiates the walk towards God and opens up the path to extraordinary possibility. Yet confession is not something you do just once to get on the path to God. Truth-telling becomes an essential daily practice in the life of the believer if one is to stay on course. Rich and varied practices of confession will be embedded in our lives if we are to reach spiritual maturity.

A RETURN TO THE CONFESSIONAL

In his remarkable spiritual memoir *Blue Like Jazz*, Donald Miller illustrates the healing power of radical confession. Miller describes an annual student festival at free-thinking Reed College in Portland, Oregon. During Ren Fayre authorities turn a blind eye for several days as Reed students carouse, drink, and get high. One year a small group of Christians met to decide what they would do during Ren Fayre. After much discussion, Miller made a comic proposal: "I said we should build a confession booth in the middle of campus and paint a sign on it that said 'Confess your sins.' I said this because I knew a lot of people would be sinning, and Christian spirituality begins by confessing our sins and repenting. I also said it was a joke. But Tony thought it was brilliant."[2] Others in the group thought it was a terrible idea to build a confessional booth in the middle of the campus bacchanal. But Tony went on to explain his version of the proposal:

> Okay, you guys....Here's the catch....We are not actually going to accept confessions....We are going to confess to them. We are going to confess that, as followers of Jesus, we have not been very loving; we have been bitter, and for that we are sorry. We will apologize for the Crusades, we will apologize for televangelists, we will apologize for neglecting the poor and the lonely, we will ask them to forgive us, and we will tell them that in our selfishness, we have misrepresented Jesus on this campus. We will tell people who come into the booth that Jesus loves them.[3]

The small group decided to go for it. Miller comments: "For so much of my life I had been defending Christianity because I thought to admit that we had done wrong was to discredit the religious system as a whole, but it isn't a religious system, it is people following Christ; and the important thing to do, the right thing to do, was to apologize for getting in the way of Jesus."[4]

In time, students drifted into the booth. The first was Jake, to whom Don gave his confession:

> Jesus said to feed the poor and to heal the sick. I have never done very much about that. Jesus said to love those who persecute me. I tend to lash out, especially if I feel threatened, you know, if my ego gets threatened. Jesus did not mix His spirituality with politics. I grew up doing that. I know that was wrong, and I know that a lot of people will not listen to the words of Christ because people like me, who know Him, carry our own agendas into the conversation rather than just relaying the message Christ wanted to get across. There's a lot more, you know.[5]

Initially befuddled, Jake became visibly moved by Don's confession. He teared up and replied, "It's all right, man." He added, "I forgive you." Miller writes: "And he meant it." Later, Jake asked, "You really believe in Jesus, don't you?" And he added, "I don't really want to become a Christian, you know, but what is that message?" Don then shared his faith with Jake. This process of confessing the sins of the church and one's individual sins went on for some time, with dozens of kids dropping by.

Confessing sins and proclaiming the Good News of Jesus in this virtual Woodstock setting is peculiar and more than a bit absurd; but it was powerful, not only for those who heard the confessions but especially for those who confessed. Miller writes: "All the people who visited the booth were grateful and gracious. I was being changed in the process....I think that night was the beginning of a change for a lot of us."6

Honest confession is life-changing, transforming those who confess (as in the case of Don Miller and his friends), and transforming those who gently receive confession. This came home to me in one of the most memorable experiences of confession in my life. Anne and I have been married for thirty-nine years. As every married person knows, you cannot be married that long and not have a lot to confess. Even with regular apologies and goodwill, injuries can mount. Sometimes they are not properly and fully dealt with. That has happened on occasion in our marriage. We are both grateful for each other and our love is deep and strong. We have weathered many storms and have grown stronger through the hard times and disappointments. Sometimes, though, the old wounds are not as healed as we thought they were.

Not long ago, we were invited to a Yom Kippur service by our friend Larry. Yom Kippur is the great Jewish feast day also known as the Day of Atonement. The service was beautiful and meaningful to us as Christians, for we too believe in atonement—our reconciliation with God and with our fellow human beings. The service was novel to us, with the liturgy of the Hebrew Bible and beautiful melodies, grand, joyous, and haunting. During Yom Kippur you are invited to consider your sins against others in the community; and, in fact, you are expected to go to members of the community and apologize for your misdeeds. At one point in the service the rabbi did something I was not prepared for. He asked everyone in the congregation to turn to someone nearby and confess his or her wrongs and to ask forgiveness. I have been a Christian for many decades, but no minister or worship leader has ever been so bold as to ask me there, in front of God and everybody, to name my wrong-doing and to ask the forgiveness of someone in the next pew. We Christians preach the idea of confession, we read scriptures about confession, but we don't generally expect Christians to practice it—at least not in such a public way.

I sat there very uncomfortably. What was I to do during this period of confession while the rabbi waited? Perhaps, I thought, being a Gentile and visitor, I would get a pass. I was not a member of this congregation. I had offended no one—at least no one on their rolls. As I sat there wondering about what I should do, Anne turned to me, and with tears in her eyes, asked: "Would you forgive me for all the ways in which I have hurt you through the years?" Immediately I protested inwardly, "No! It is I that have so much to ask your forgiveness for!" But I didn't protest. Overwhelmed by a face that radiated earnestness and love, all I could say was, feebly, "Yes, I forgive you. And please forgive me too."

God, I have found, has a grand sense of humor. Why did I have to go to a Jewish synagogue for such a moving experience of confession and forgiveness? As the Gospel of Mark teaches, faith is often found in unexpected places—often not in the usual holy places we expect. And so I encountered God's grace in the rites of Yom Kippur, my own Day of Atonement. That experience also got me to thinking. What if Christians began to see each day and certainly each First Day of the Week as their day of atonement? What if Yom Kippur is the right idea, but we just need it more often than once a year? What if Christians came to the assembly expecting to lay down their burdens, their griefs, and their grievances before each other? What if they refused to go forward with their worship and their countless religious activities until they had made amends with their brothers and sisters in the faith? Jesus taught us that if a brother or a sister has a complaint against us, we are to leave our gift at the altar and be reconciled before we continue to worship. Could it be that our congregations are unnecessarily burdened by pain because we have failed to confess our faults one to another?

The pilgrim heart is a confessing heart, one that lives vibrantly in community where the truth is bravely shared and kindly received. When wrong is committed, it is freely confessed and graciously forgiven. Yet, to tell the truth, I have spent long periods of my life where I neither offered a confession nor received the honest confession of another. It is possible, in fact, in many churches never to hear a confession, to offer a confession, or to receive absolution. This is passing strange, given the ample instruction of Scripture:

> Therefore confess your sins to one another, and pray for one another, so
> that you may be healed. (James 5:16)
>
> If we say that we have no sin, we deceive ourselves, and the truth is not in
> us. If we confess our sins, he who is faithful and just will forgive us our sins
> and cleanse us from all unrighteousness. (1 John 1:8-9)
>
> While I kept silence, my body wasted away through my groaning all day
> long. For day and night your hand was heavy upon me; my strength was
> dried up as by the heat of summer. Then I acknowledged my sin to you,
> and I did not hide my iniquity; I said, "I will confess my transgressions to
> the Lord," and you forgave the guilt of my sin. (Psalm 32:3-5)
>
> No one who conceals transgressions will prosper, but one who confesses
> and forsakes them will obtain mercy. (Proverbs 28:13)

The point is clear. The concealment of transgression produces illness (both spiritual and physical), while truth-telling brings healing.

Through the centuries, Christian believers have understood the centrality of confessing transgressions and receiving forgiveness (which is called "absolution"). Healthy faith requires both confession and absolution—individually, in small groups, and in the assembly. Yet confession is practiced erratically and sporadically at best, even among churches purporting to follow Scriptural teaching closely. In many Protestant churches, the corporate confession of sin is expressed during the worship liturgy, but formal pronouncements of absolution are rarely heard. Even in churches which have formalized confession and absolution through established liturgies of confession and the institution of the confessional, "going to confession" has fallen into general neglect. Why is this?

Christianity is most powerful when it is fearless about truth. Our faith boldly proclaims that *God is truth.* Christ is full of "grace and truth" (John 1:14), the embodiment of truth (John 14:6). God's commandments are truth (Psalm 119:142, 151), and believers are promised that the Holy Spirit, the Spirit of truth, will live within them and guide them (John 16:13). Followers of Christ, then, are to be bold in their truth-telling: "So then, putting away falsehood, let all of us speak the truth to our neighbor, for we are members of one another" (Ephesians 4:25). It is right to expect Christians to be famous for the passion for truth-telling, and this applies above all to the truth about themselves. They are not willing to settle for the cheap righteousness that comes from exalting themselves above their fallen neighbors. Rather, in the words of novelist Mary Gordon, they "give up the exhilaration of [their] unassailable righteousness," confessing that they are sinners in the hands of a merciful God.

Few spiritual practices more powerfully shape us into the image of Christ than regular, honest confession of our specific sins before another disciple of Jesus. This is because confession does several remarkable, soul-changing things in us. First, it challenges our pride. In the words of Bonhoeffer, confession before another believer breaks open "the last stronghold of self-justification. The sinner surrenders; he gives up all his evil." The difficulty of such a confession is that it is a humiliation requiring a kind of death to self. "It hurts, it cuts a man down, it is a dreadful blow to pride. To stand there before a brother as a sinner is an ignominy that is almost unbearable....Because this humiliation is so hard we continually scheme to evade confessing to a brother."[7]

Yet when we confess to a safe, reliable, and spiritually mature person, it changes us and our relationship to God and the community. Confession ends our terrible isolation from God and from our brothers and sisters in the faith. Hidden sin, as Bonhoeffer observes, makes a sham of fellowship.[8] I can recall several occasions when I thought I was in close fellowship with a brother or a sister, only to discover later that he or she was carrying a terrible burden, a heavy darkness, that he or she refused to share or discuss. The sense of hurt, sadness, and even betrayal was very deep, once the secret burden became known. How different, and how much superior, our relationship would have been had the truth been shared safely in community. When sin is confessed its power is dramatically diminished. There is, of course, danger in confessing to improper people at improper times. Jesus taught us to take care not to cast what is most precious before those who will treat it unworthily or with contempt (Matthew 7:6). Fortunately, a considerable body of literature is available to help us rediscover and establish the good practice of confession.[9]

Christianity is much more than thinking right thoughts about God. It consists of much more than "mental acts." It is preeminently a social religion. It involves practices that include others. Confession is a superb example of this social dimension. It is a gift offered by one person to another. Many understand this, of course, when it comes to private confession—that is, confession of our sins to God. The Psalms present a vivid picture of the individual sinner before God: "Have mercy on me, O God, according to your steadfast love; according to your abundant mercy blot out my transgressions. Wash me thoroughly from my iniquity, and cleanse me from my sin" (Psalm 51:1). This picture of the broken and contrite heart prostrate before God speaks powerfully to most Christians.

Richard Foster offers an excellent overview of the prayer of "examen," as it is called, a prayer in which we ask God to stir up an awareness of our sin. In this prayer we ask him to test us, search us, and know our hearts (Psalm 139:1). We grant to God all that we are, our virtues and our failures. We expose the shadows of our hearts freely and openly to God.[10] There are many other ways to express one's spiritual need to God: through journaling (where the writer carries out a spiritual inventory), through the reading of Scripture (for example, praying biblical prayers of confession like Psalm 51), through meditating on the Lord's Prayer or other written prayers, through private retreats, and so forth. Whichever approach we embrace, confession must be at the center of the pilgrim heart.

In an age which tends to view religion as primarily a private matter, an intimate transaction between the individual and one's God, many are comfortable only with private confession. Jesus did teach us to go to our private quarters to pray, but Scripture also clearly teaches that confession is not solely a "private matter" between the worshiper and the deity. Private prayer and private confession are necessary but insufficient. Private prayer runs certain risks. In our solo prayers we can fool ourselves. We can think we are yielding, when we are going only half-way. We can let ourselves off too easily, not fully intending to mend our ways or be fully accountable. More is needed.

The Bible teaches public and shared confession. Jesus, for example, in the model prayer is replete with plural pronouns, "*Our* Father in heaven....Give *us* this day *our* daily bread. And forgive *us our* debts, as *we* also have forgiven *our* debtors" (Matthew 6:9-13, my emphasis). When the church came into being in Acts 2, its first activity was a general group repentance and confession. All in the assembly were cut to the heart and said so. Even the Psalms that at first glance look individualistic, aren't really so. In fact, a prayer like Psalm 51 has functioned as a communal prayer in Jewish and Christian congregations for millennia. Further evidence of the communal nature of confession comes from James who instructs: "confess your sins to one another, and pray for one another, so that you may be healed" (James 5:16).

Twenty centuries later we must still find appropriate and effective ways to confess to one another, and therein lies a challenge. In large assemblies, where Christians may not have meaningful relationships, and where they may not even know one another, "public confession" is deeply problematic. Such venues are not necessarily spiritually or psychologically safe. The chances of abuse, embarrassment, and misunderstanding are considerable. In such settings, the recitation of established confessional prayers, such as Psalm 51 or the Lord's Prayer, can be especially helpful. This prayer from *The Book of Common Prayer* forcefully expresses sentiments of the contrite worshiper:

> Most merciful God,
> we confess that we have sinned against you
> in thought, word, and deed,
> by what we have done,
> and by what we have left undone.
> We have not loved you with our whole heart;
> we have not loved our neighbors as ourselves.

We are truly sorry and we humbly repent.

For the sake of your Son Jesus Christ,

have mercy on us and forgive us;

that we may delight in your will,

and walk in your ways,

to the glory of your Name. Amen.[11]

Such general confessions can be effective, but I do not think they are all sufficient. They don't constitute the full, individual confession that each of us needs. A much more likely setting for this is in a small group where people have covenanted together to tell the truth about their lives, in safety and in confidentiality. Such small gatherings can lead to remarkable levels of community and transformative change. Furthermore, when one has an authentic soul-friend, as described in chapter 7, one always has a worthy and safe confessor.

CONFESSION AND ABSOLUTION

Confession is not only to be heard, forgiveness is to be received. As we speak our failures freely, it is with a longing to hear something in reply. We want to know that our sins have, indeed, been forgiven. "Absolution" (Latin *ab* + *solvere* "to loosen, release") is the pronouncement of the glorious truth that we have been released from our burden. We should not underestimate our need to hear the words that declare our freedom from sin. While some may view this as an unnecessary (or even a dangerous) ritual, all Christians ought to hear (and hear frequently) that God is a good and gracious God, ready to forgive, ready to welcome them home. While it is true that only God forgives, it is also true that we can benefit from hearing divine forgiveness explicitly pronounced. We can say, "Almighty God have mercy on you, forgive you all your sins through our Lord Jesus Christ, strengthen you in all goodness, and by the power of the Holy Spirit keep you in eternal life," as the *Book of Common Prayer* expresses it. We can say over one another, "God's promises are faithful and true. He has promised to forgive all who repent. You have been forgiven through the power of Jesus Christ. Amen." Or we can quote Scripture on the point: "He who is faithful and just will forgive us our sins and cleanse us from all unrighteousness" (1 John 1:9); "Your sins are forgiven on account of his name" (1 John 2:12); "Take heart, my son [and daughter]; your sins are forgiven" (Matthew 9:2).

In our personal relationships, we understand that confession requires, even demands, an overt response from a listener. To receive only silence after confession is potentially dangerous. Imagine what it would be like to pour out a confession to someone you had greatly injured; but after your painful apology, all you received from your listener was stony silence. How would you feel? Would you think the process of confession was complete or successful? Not likely. Yet many worshipers go to church regularly, repenting of their sins week after week—through scripture, song, and prayer—expecting to hear nothing in reply. They depart with the same heavy burden that they carried into the assembly. This might change if they could hear these words spoken boldly and with great conviction, "Take heart, my children; your sins are forgiven; go now in peace." Do we have the right to speak such words? Yes, because Christ has called us to speak his words of truth to others. We can emphatically affirm that Christ receives and forgives penitent people.

While it is true that some churches make absolution the special privilege of the clergy, the ability to pronounce absolution belongs to all the followers of Jesus. We hear each other's confession (James 5:16), and we pronounce God's forgiveness to one another, not because of our special power or status, but because of the promise of Scripture that Christ forgives the penitent. This is why Jesus said, "If you forgive the sins of any, they are forgiven them; if you retain the sins of any, they are retained" (John 20:23; cf. Matthew 18:18).

CONCLUSION

The pilgrim heart is a confessing heart. The followers of Jesus honor him as the embodiment of Truth, and so, more than anything, they want to be truthful about their lives. Such honesty is transforming and disarming. It not only strengthens the individual believer, but it builds strong ties within the community. Countless congregations have endured painful division because their members were not truly confessional with one another. Unconfessed sins of selfishness, jealousy, envy, and pride have decimated families, churches, and whole societies. On the other hand, when people trust Christ's own words, when they bravely confess their trespasses and humbly forgive the trespasses of others, they make way for the possibility of miraculous changes in relationships.

Confession is a joint process involving a sincere speaker and an attentive, responsive listener. The confessor speaks his or her weakness; but the speaker must be heard, held, and loved by someone—first and foremost by God, but also by a brother or a sister who embodies the patience of Christ. In receiving another's confession, we are neither fixer nor therapist. Richard Foster suggests that we need not endlessly carry the burdens of others. Rather,

> we release them into the arms of the Father. Without this releasing the burdens will become too much for us, and depression will set in. Besides, it is not necessary. Our task in reality is a small one: to hold the agony of others just long enough for them to let go of it for themselves. Then together we can give all things over to God.[12]

9

FORGIVING: THE LOVE
THAT TRAVELS FARTHER

And forgive us our debts, as we also have forgiven our debtors.
Matthew 6:12

Forgiveness itself is a form of suffering.
—Miroslav Volf

While they were stoning Stephen, he prayed,
"...Lord, do not hold this sin against them."
Acts 7:59-60

During the Iranian Islamic Revolution, Hassan Dehqani-Tafti, a Christian, was fleeing the country with his family. On the way to the airport, members of the Revolutionary Guard stopped the family, dragged Hassan's son, Bahram, from the car, and murdered him. After this great tragedy, the grieving father was somehow able to utter this prayer:

O God

We remember not only our son but also his murderers;

Not because they killed him in the prime of his youth and made our hearts bleed and our tears flow,

Not because with this savage act they have brought further disgrace on the name of our country among the civilized nations of the world;

But because through their crime we now follow thy footsteps more
    closely in the way of sacrifice.

The terrible fire of this calamity burns up all selfishness and
    possessiveness in us;

Its flame reveals the depth of depravity and meanness and
    suspicion, the dimension of hatred and the measure of
    sinfulness in human nature;

It makes obvious as never before our need to trust in God's love
    as shown in the cross of Jesus and his resurrection;

Love which makes us free from hate towards our persecutors;

Love which brings patience, forbearance, courage, loyalty, humility,
    generosity, greatness of heart;

Love which more than ever deepens our trust in God's final victory
    and his eternal designs for the Church and for the world;

Love which teaches us how to prepare ourselves to face our own day
    of death.

O God

Our son's blood has multiplied the fruit of the Spirit in the soil
    of our souls;

So when his murderers stand before thee on the day of judgment

Remember the fruit of the Spirit by which they have enriched
    our lives.

And forgive.[1]

This prayer is remarkable, perhaps even shocking. How many of us, after the
murder of a loved one, could pray such words? Yet, considered in the light of the
lives of the great believers through the ages, perhaps one of the most remarkable
things about Hassan's prayer is how unremarkable it is. This prayer is but an
extension of Jesus' prayer spoken from the cross, "Father, forgive them; for they do
not know what they are doing" (Luke 23:34). It is the prayer of Stephen, the first
Christian martyr, "Lord, do not hold this sin against them" (Acts 7:60). It was the

prayer of the first Christian prince of Kiev, who was executed by his own brother in 1015: "Lord Jesus Christ, who came to this world as a man and suffered your passion, allowing your hands to be nailed to the cross for our sins, give me the strength to endure my passion. It comes not from my enemies, but from my own brother: Yet, Lord, do not account it to him as sin."[2] Likewise it is the prayer of Michael Pro, who died before a firing squad in Mexico on November 23, 1927: "Lord, you know I am innocent. I forgive my enemies with all my heart. Hail, Christ our King."[3]

Jesus taught us to love our enemies, and an essential expression of authentic love is forgiveness: We are forgiven by God, Jesus teaches us in his prayer, *because we have forgiven others* (Matthew 6:12). Indeed, forgiveness by God is the only petition in the Lord's Prayer that is conditional. Jesus is clear on this point. After offering the model prayer, Jesus explains: "For if you forgive others their trespasses, your heavenly Father will also forgive you; but if you do not forgive others, neither will your Father forgive your trespasses" (6:14-15). Jesus says elsewhere: "Whenever you stand praying, forgive, *if you have anything against anyone*; so that your Father in heaven may also forgive you your trespasses" (Mark 11:25, my emphasis). The Apostle Paul reiterates the unbroken link between granting forgiveness and receiving forgiveness: "forgive each other; just as the Lord has forgiven you, so you also must forgive" (Colossians 3:13; cf. Ephesians 4:32). The reciprocal giving and receiving of forgiveness is one of the central features of the Christian faith, surely one of the most challenging, *kenotic* dimensions of our faith. It stands at the heart of the gospel, an expression of the extreme demands of love made visible in the cross where we see the manifestation of loving forgiveness. It proclaims: Jesus came to forgive; we have been forgiven by him; we must forgive others. Nothing is more basic or more radical:

> We instinctively reach for a shield and a sword, but the cross offers us outstretched arms and a naked body with a pierced side; we feel we need the cunning wisdom of serpents, but the cross invites us to the foolishness of innocent doves.[4]

And so we renounce our natural, reflexive tendency to protect or attack. We obey the lesson of the broken body on a cross. Is there any truth harder to absorb than this one? Is there any lesson more needful in our time?

FORGIVENESS: IS IT POSSIBLE?

We forgive because we follow in Jesus' steps. His example is ours: "For to this you have been called, because Christ also suffered for you, leaving you an example, so that you should follow in his steps" (1 Peter 2:21). Ever moved by "the inconceivable self-emptying of God in the events of Good Friday and Holy Saturday,"[5] we extend grace to people who wrong us. Through Christ's prayer from the cross, as Moltmann observes, "the universal law of retaliation is annulled. In the name of the Crucified, from now on only forgiveness holds sway. Christianity...is a religion of reconciliation."[6] A great deal is hidden in the amazing call to forgive. It is not only right to forgive; in it we will find our healing, individually and communally.

Ira Byock is a physician who has spent much of his life caring for patients near the end of their lives. Director of palliative medicine at the Dartmouth Hitchcock Medical Center, Dr. Byock is an authority on the care of the terminally ill. Through the years he has seen something that brings relief, release, and transformation among dying patients and their loved ones. In his book *The Four Things That Matter Most*, he identifies the basic messages that people most need to speak and hear as they face death. (The truth is, these messages need to be spoken and heard throughout everyone's life, not only at the end.) The four messages are: Please forgive me. I forgive you. Thank you. And, I love you.[7]

It is noteworthy that of all the possible messages necessary at the point of death, two of them concern forgiveness. It is not hard to understand why. The failure to give and receive forgiveness produces untold misery at the microcosmic and the macrocosmic levels. Unforgiven, people live with endless shame and regret, with unresolved resentment and anger. Without forgiveness, families dissolve, marriages fail, churches split, and nations divide. On the other hand, the giving and receiving of forgiveness releases people from the crushing burden of hostility, bitterness, and anger. Forgiveness, indeed, is an essential nutrient of the soul. It is "a passage to a sanctuary of wholeness, that nurturing place where we feel intimately connected to the people who matter most to us. It is a place of healing and transformation."[8] Forgiveness may be the one miracle that we can experience daily, if we are but willing to risk our pride and renounce our need to be "right."

WHERE DOES FORGIVENESS BEGIN?

Though followers of Jesus know that they need to give and receive forgiveness, they often balk at actually practicing it. When we contemplate the deepest hurts in our hearts, some that we may have carried for decades, the objections to pardoning others are many. How does one forgive the one who has abused him or her physically, emotionally, sexually? Isn't forgiveness a cheapening of the injury? Isn't forgiveness—especially of the unrepentant—an act of injustice that compounds the original wrong? The answer to these questions is no. Forgiveness in New Testament terms never trivializes the injury, no matter how small or grave. "Beloved, never avenge yourselves," writes Paul, who teaches us to leave the judgment to God. "Do not repay anyone evil for evil, but take thought for what is noble in the sight of all" (Romans 12:17, 19). For the sake of our own well being, we must transcend the desire for retaliation. There is a better place to stand, where we are blessed and free from pain. Consider the following points a kind of primer on a very complex subject.

First, we should consider that forgiveness is a grace that begins with God, not with us. It does not flow from our own creativity, energy, or muscular wills. The capacity to pardon derives from our own Rescuer, the one who—while we were yet hopelessly lost—gave himself for us (Romans 5:8). Forgiveness begins beneath the cross.

For centuries Christians have placed a great deal of emphasis upon the cross—not just upon the theological meaning of the event, but the contemplation of and reflection upon the physical and spiritual dimensions of the crucifixion. The cross inspired deep emotion. By design crosses and altar paintings such as Matthias Grünewald's or sculptures like Michelangelo's multiple *pietás* stirred a sense of wonder and awe at the costliness of redemption. But these meditations on the cross also reminded the worshipers of their lowly status before God. Bonhoeffer says it well:

> Anybody who lives beneath the Cross and who has discerned in the Cross
> of Jesus the utter wickedness of all men and of his own heart will find
> there is no sin that can ever be alien to him. Anybody who has once been
> horrified by the dreadfulness of his own sin that nailed Jesus to the Cross
> will no longer be horrified by even the rankest sins of a brother. Looking

> at the Cross of Jesus, he knows the human heart....In daily, earnest living
> with the Cross of Christ the Christian loses the spirit of human censori-
> ousness on the one hand and weak indulgence on the other...."[9]

Forgiveness is amazingly difficult at times, given the horrors and the injuries we may undergo. Yet forgiveness becomes comprehensible in the shadow of the cross which transmutes our situation, giving us clarity about our own neediness and failure. C. S. Lewis seems to have had this in mind when he confessed that the "true Christian's nostril is to be continually attentive to the inner cess-pool" of one's own heart.[10]

SEEING THE PATTERN IN THE MOSAIC

Another way that it becomes possible for us to practice forgiveness is to imagine the great design of our lives. Frederick Buechner tells the tragic story of his father's suicide when Frederick was ten years old. The family had no religious faith when Buechner's father died. There was no funeral, no memorial, and even worse, there was rarely any mention of the father again. The suicide became a dreadful family secret, and the silence profoundly wounded the young boy. Yet, as Buechner's story unfolded, that tragic event became one element in a long sequence of events that eventually led Buechner to faith. He subsequently became a minister, a fine novelist, and arguably one of the greatest Christian authors of our day. Buechner explains:

> I believe that we are all called to see that the day-by-day lives of all of us—
> the things that happened long ago, the things that happened only this
> morning—are also hallowed and crucial and part of a great drama in which
> souls are lost and souls are saved including our own.[11]

Buechner is quite careful to say that he does not attribute the death of his father to some cruel divine plan. God did not will the suicide of his father. But Buechner does believe that "God is present in [the tragic events of our lives] not as their cause but as the one who even in the hardest and most hair-raising of them offers us the possibility of that new life and healing which I believe is what salvation is."[12] For Buechner, God is the author of history, and he continues to work in history, including the plots of our own lives:

> ...in everything that has happened to us over the years God was offering us

possibilities of new life and healing which, though we may have missed
them at the time, we can still choose and be brought to life by and healed
by all these years later.

According to Buechner, memory makes it possible for us to bless our past. Through
it he could "see how God's mercy was for me buried deep even in my father's
death...."[13] Buechner was able through this large perspective to forgive God (for
letting his father kill himself), to forgive his father (for abandoning him), and even
to forgive himself.

This is, of course, a familiar theme of Scripture and well illustrated by the
remarkable story of Joseph. As a young man, Joseph was rejected by his jealous
brothers who sold him into slavery. He was later mistreated in Egypt by Potiphar's
wife, enduring a long and unjust imprisonment. But by the final chapter of the
story, Joseph is able to perceive the design. The brothers are in mortal fear as they
stand before their wronged brother: "What if Joseph still bears a grudge against us
and pays us back in full for all the wrong that we did to him?" the brothers ask
themselves (Genesis 50:15). But Joseph replies, "Do not be afraid! Am I in the place
of God? Even though you intended to do harm to me, God intended it for good, in
order to preserve a numerous people, as he is doing today. So have no fear; I myself
will provide for you and your little ones" (50:19-21). Joseph understood what the
great Danish writer Isak Dinesen once wrote: "Life is a mosaic work of the Lord's,
which he keeps filling in bit by bit."[14] When a person is injured, she must take into
account the larger picture, as does one of Dinesen's characters, Babette, who was
denied the opportunity to fully exercise her natural gifts: "'Yet this is not the end. I feel,
Babette, that this is not the end. In Paradise you will be the great artist that God meant
you to be! Ah!' she added, the tears streaming down her cheek. 'Ah, how you will
enchant the angels!'"

Mature believers eventually learn the same lesson that Joseph learned. With
Dinesen and Buechner they affirm that only the final chapter of a life can explain or
illuminate the pain, the misfortune, and the suffering of the earlier events of our
lives. "The sad things of long ago," says Buechner, "will remain part of who we are,"
but they will cease to be "a burden of guilt, recrimination, and regret" when we

finally recognize the pattern of meaning in our lives. All this we shall see is true, if we are willing to go through the peculiar *kenotic* pain of letting go, of abandoning our role as judge and jury, of needing to get even. When we can recite the words of Romans 8:28 with conviction, "We know that all things work together for good for those who love God...," then we will enter a realm of amazing freedom. Then we will say with Lady Julian of Norwich: "All will be well, all manner of things will be well."

FORGIVING OURSELVES

One of the great impediments to forgiving others is the difficulty of absolving ourselves. Often we feel bad about what we have done or left undone, but rather than confess it, we carry our guilt and shame, and it becomes transmuted into anger towards others. As Lewis Smedes observes: "We do not have to be bad persons to do bad things. If only bad people did bad things to other people we would live in a pretty good world. We hurt people by our bungling as much as we do by our vices."[15] Ironically, our very decency—our desire to be "good people"—can compound our capacity to hurt others. Smedes observes shrewdly, "the more decent we are the more acutely we feel our pain for the unfair hurts we caused. Our pain becomes our hate. *The pain we cause other people becomes the hate we feel for ourselves.* For having done them wrong. We judge, we convict, and sentence ourselves. Mostly in secret."[16]

Horton Foote's play *Habitation of Dragons* is an extraordinary story of what happens to a family in which the family's self-inflicted injuries are chronic and pervasive, but also where there has been a general failure to offer or receive forgiveness. The sadness and the hurt are excruciating. Near the end of the play, the aged Virgil, tragically burdened by the guilt of his own wrongdoing towards his siblings, tries to fathom what has happened to his extended family. In the final scene he comes to discover the necessity of forgiveness, including the necessity of forgiving himself. He recalls a dream:

> Once when I was still in South Texas I had this dream. It was just as plain
> to me. I dreamt I was a boy still, eight or nine, and this Preacher was there
> and I was crying, and he kept saying, "Forgiveness." That's all he said.

Forgiveness. And I woke up to tell my mama and papa about the dream, and of course, they weren't there. No one was there, and I was alone. Who was there to forgive? Forgiveness. That's all he said. But what was there to forgive, except myself, or ask forgiveness of? Nobody. Nobody except myself.[17]

Since "none is righteous, no, not one," healing comes when we recognize that we are not outside the set of sinners, that we have failed time and time again, and will fail again—yet God's grace is sufficient, even for us.

FORGIVENESS, THE MIRACLE

Many questions remain when we consider the urgent and under-practiced blessing of forgiveness. How do we forgive the unreachable and the unrepentant? How do we reconcile forgiveness with our longing for justice? Does forgiveness erase the possibility of penalty or consequences? How do we forgive the unrepentant "monsters"? These and many other questions emerge when we take seriously the call to forgive. Thankfully, there is a good deal of literature on the subject.[18]

Forgiveness seems unfair at times; but the mountains of alienation, death, and destruction that accrue from undiminished anger are far more unfair. In the words of Reinhold Niebuhr: "We must finally be reconciled with our foe, lest we both perish in the vicious cycle of hatred."[19] Vengeance never settles the matter. The Gospel way can, however, end the cycle of violence. Jesus and the great saints point the way to *shalom*, which is never easy because forgiveness is counterintuitive and "against our nature." The romance of forgiveness evaporates as soon as it becomes our turn to practice it. C. S. Lewis wryly observes, "Everyone says forgiveness is a lovely idea, until they have something to forgive." But pardoning others and ourselves is the pilgrim heart's difficult path to wholeness and health. William Blake was right: "The glory of Christianity is to conquer by forgiveness."

10

LISTENING: WITHIN THE DEEP STREAM OF SILENCE

The Lord is in his holy temple; let all the earth keep silence before him.
Habakkuk 2:20

If you love truth, be a lover of silence.
—Isaac of Niniveh

The pilgrim heart is an attentive heart, one skilled at screening out the endless chatter, the distracting ambient "white noise" of daily existence. For the faithful follower of Jesus it is necessary, at times, to escape what Thomas Merton excoriates as "the general meaninglessness of countless slogans and clichés repeated over and over again so that in the end one listens without hearing and responds without thinking."[1] Only by entering the pastoral silence, beside the "still waters," can we hear the astonishing and unequivocal voice of the Good Shepherd: "My sheep hear my voice. I know them, and they follow me" (John 10:27). It might seem elementary that a follower of Jesus should look for ways to hear the voice of the Master, but we do not easily topple the thick barriers to attentive listening.

LEARNING TO ATTEND

To hear the voice of the Lord God must be very difficult; otherwise, it's hard to account for the hundreds of verses in Scripture which exhort us to hear. Most notable of these is the *shema* (Hebrew for "hear"), which lies at the heart of Jewish worship: "Hear, O Israel: The Lord is our God, the Lord alone" (Deuteronomy 6:4). A capacity to hear God is a longed for spiritual gift in the Jewish (and Christian) traditions. For this reason Jewish boys have for centuries often been named "Simon, "Simeon," or "Shimon"—variations of the Hebrew word for "hear" or "hearing." (Imagine a child today being named "Listen Up!" or "I Hear You!")

C. S. Lewis once noted two truths about our desire to meet God. The first truth is that God makes himself available to us in many ways, and the second is that we still fail to detect him. In other words, God shows up and we look the other way. Lewis writes:

> We may ignore, but we can nowhere evade, the presence of God. The world
> is crowded with Him. He walks everywhere *incognito*. And the *incognito* is not
> always hard to penetrate. The real labour is to remember, to attend. In fact,
> to come awake. Still more, to remain awake.[2]

The key word here is "attend," for at the core of the word is the notion of stretching or straining to achieve something. Attending requires genuine effort. "To attend" means to wait patiently for, to direct one's mind and energies towards something, to live expectantly. This is why John Milton could write of those who humbly attend on God as being truly faithful: "they also serve who only stand and wait." There is understatement here as "only standing and waiting" may encompass years, including long periods of suffering, doubt, and tears. Thus, "remaining awake" is not a state of passive idleness, but its antithesis. Attending is the heroic spiritual posture of one who is fully present and eager to meet God, whether at the office, on the freeway, or on the mountain top.

Lewis observes further that we miss God's presence not only because we are distracted or inattentive, but because we do not offer the Lord a suitable welcome. Conflicted hosts, we shun the guest as we call out to him. Even as we ask, "Where is God? Why has he abandoned me?" we yet may evade him because we actually fear what his presence will mean: "For he comes not only to raise up," writes Lewis, "but to cast down; to deny, to rebuke, to interrupt." God's presence, to put it mildly, is inconvenient.

The situation is not unlike our relationships with ordinary mortals. Why do husbands fail to hear their wives? Why do children fail to hear their parents, or friends each other? Listening demands much of us. It requires cooperation, investment, and the passionate attention of both parties. Could it be that our sense of God's absence is partly our doing? Have we offered him a sincere and robust welcome? Have we prepared the way for his coming? Have we prepared ourselves for his coming? Just as there is discipline to all enterprises (whether it is reading, listening to a symphony, painting a picture, or playing a sport), so also there is a discipline to meeting God. Scripture and thousands of years of spiritual practice teach a great deal about the "courtesies" that go with meeting God, and we would do well to learn them. One of these courtesies is attentive listening.

Elijah's remarkable encounter with God is illustrative. In flight from his mortal enemy Jezebel, depressed and desperately forsaken (so it seemed to him), Elijah retreated to Mount Horeb. And there in solitude he heard a voice: "Go out and stand on the mountain before the Lord, for the Lord is about to pass by" (1 Kings 19:11). Elijah did so, and he was treated to a magnificent light-and-sound show that would have astonished a Las Vegas impresario:

> Now there was a great wind, so strong that it was splitting mountains and
> breaking rocks in pieces before the Lord, but the Lord was not in the wind;
> and after the wind an earthquake, but the Lord was not in the earthquake;
> and after the earthquake a fire, but the Lord was not in the fire; and after
> the fire a sound of sheer silence. (19:11-12)

Elijah met God, not in dazzling special effects, but in a way no movie director or rock musician could imagine. The Lord of the universe came to Elijah in the ensuing silence. The Hebrew phrase found in 19:12—rendered as "a sound of sheer silence" or as "a still small voice"—presents a difficult challenge to the translator. How does one convey the paradox and the mystery implicit in this phrase? What is a "sound" of "silence"? What is this speaking silence, this "thin voice of silence," as one commentator renders it? We are stretching towards a mysterious reality, quite beyond anything the cleverest communicator can devise.

TWO KINDS OF SILENCE

Most people understand one kind of silence: a negative silence signifying emptiness, abandonment, or relational failure, when one hopes for a message (an expression of love, an apology, a blessing) but receives none. Yet "the silent treatment" is not the only possibility. There is another kind of silence, a positive stillness honored throughout Scripture. This second kind of silence is, paradoxically, a positive form of communication. It is seen in the quiet communion of lover and beloved when words become superfluous. It is felt in the whispers of a mother as she consoles her child. It is known in the resonant hush as one walks alone in nature. Potentially, there is spiritual meaning in these kinds of silence. Elijah encountered a speaking silence, a silence so pregnant that it pulsed with the presence of the Holy One of Israel. Wherever this silence is found, it can lead to awareness of God:

"Be still, and know that I am God!" (Psalm 46:10)

"Be silent before the Lord God!" (Zephaniah 1:7)

"But the Lord is in his holy temple; let all the earth keep silence before him!" (Habakkuk 2:20)

 "Never be rash with your mouth, nor let your heart be quick to utter a word before God, for God is in heaven, and you upon earth; therefore let your words be few." (Ecclesiastes 5:2)

Through the centuries spiritually mature disciples have known the necessity of this kind of silence. Søren Kierkegaard once observed that people commonly suppose that the most important thing in prayer is to concentrate upon what one is praying for:

Yet in the true, eternal sense it is just the reverse: the true relation in prayer is not when God hears what is prayed for, but when the person praying continues to pray until he is the one who hears, who hears what God wills. The "immediate" person, therefore...makes demands in his prayers; the true man of prayer only attends.[3]

It may well be that the deepest form of prayer begins when we run out of things to say. Remembering Jesus' prayer vigils, we might consider whether Jesus actually delivered a continuous monologue throughout the night, or whether he might have contemplated and listened as well. Listening prayer may also explain why the prayers of Jesus recorded in the Gospels—even the one in John 17—are not very long. Perhaps Jesus' prayer vigils were marked by periods of intense listening for the will of God.

WELCOMING SILENCE

The rewards of silence are considerable. Attentive silence makes relationship with God possible, for all healthy relationships involve careful listening. André Neher explains, "The inescapable condition of hearing is silence, and whoever is not silent while another speaks is not in a dialogic situation." Psychologist Raymond Carpentier observes:

> Dialogue, when it is really open to the other, when it is a goodwill that is not some vague expectation but an active desire to receive, to listen, to seek to go out of oneself, and to admit the universe of another, could not proceed to its ultimate conclusions without the sacrifice of one of the partners....Truly to engage in a dialogue would be to question one's own being through the information that comes from another....True dialogue is sacrifice....[4]

Most of us have observed the scene, sometimes comic, often sad, when two people speak at each other simultaneously—without either doing any listening. Whatever this is, it is not effective dialogue. Communication is possible only when the partners are able to listen wholeheartedly, which is to say that true communication can occur only if partners willingly become silent. This requires a renunciation or effacement of the self. It is more than the meeting of "two mental worlds," says Carpentier. It is "the sacrifice of two partners ready to throw themselves open to the creation."

While Carpentier is writing as a secular psychologist about ordinary relationships, the principles he articulates have a spiritual application. Healthy relationships require the cessation of chatter and one's need to be correct. Moving into deep spiritual communion calls for patience and kenotic surrender.

The thought of radical relinquishment may give us pause. Communion with the Other is not cheap or easy. If Christ went to the cross to communicate divine love to us, what will it cost us? It is painful to go silent, to abandon the cacophonies of our daily routines, and to wait patiently. But, of course, the rewards to be found on the other side of the silence are considerable: "Be still and know that I am God." "It is good to wait in silence for the salvation of God" (Lamentations 3:26).

FINDING OTHERS IN SILENCE

Not only does entry into silence potentially lead us to God; it can dramatically improve our relationship with others. By temporarily banishing the various forms of noise from our lives, we can learn something essential about ourselves and our neighbors. Listening sharpens our understanding, stirs our compassion, and empowers us to care for others. Periods of retreat, as seen in Scripture, are often preludes to world-changing ministry. Perhaps this is why so many of the Bible's great spiritual leaders (Moses, Elijah, John the Baptist, Paul, and Jesus) spent time in the desert. "Desert spirituality" is the name for this practice of extended retreat marked by intense prayer, fasting, immersion in Scripture, and meditation. Those unfamiliar with desert spirituality often view retreat as escapist and selfish; but authentic retreat is not about "world-flight." It is, rather, preparation for service to the world. It is a discipline of the heart to end the world's domination of our thoughts, a challenge to the tyranny of "group think," mindless sloganeering, and commercial indoctrination. Retreat liberates us from the "constant din of empty words and machine noises, the endless booming of loudspeakers" that make "true communication and true communion almost impossible," Thomas Merton observes.[5]

By restoring the divine perspective, solitude frees us from pervasive cultural manipulations and enables us to care again. Merton explains: "Without an element of solitude there can be no compassion because when a man is lost in the wheels of a social machine he is no longer aware of human needs as a matter of personal responsibility."[6] Thus, the experience of the quiet is a means to love and heal the world's wounds, not an escape from responsibility. Henri Nouwen is wonderfully clear on this point:

> Once you have spent time on the mountain or in the desert, you can go into this world and touch people, heal them, speak with them, and make them aware that they are beloved, chosen, and blessed. When you discover your belovedness by God, you see the belovedness of other people and call that forth. It's an incredible mystery of God's love that the more you know how

deeply you are loved, the more you will see how deeply your sisters and
your brothers in the human family are loved.[7]

As its practitioners have proven through the centuries, solitude is true service to others. Merton advises: "Go into the desert not to escape [others] but in order to find them in God." Chaim Potok, the great novelist, makes much the same point: "In the silence between us, [we] hear the world crying."

FINDING OURSELVES IN SILENCE

Nouwen once pronounced a judgment that has often rung in my ear. He said, "People in the West are very sophisticated, but they know very little about the movements of the Spirit in us." Technologically advanced, we are primitives when it comes to soul-care. Just as we can stuff our bodies with fast food yet languish from poor nourishment; so also, if we fill our lives with noise, we risk starving ourselves of the "peace that passes understanding." In the silence you can get your soul back, your sense of self. Nouwen explains:

> Why is it so important that you are with God and God alone on the mountain top? It's important because it's the place in which you can listen to the voice of the One who calls you the beloved. To pray is to listen to the One who calls you "my beloved daughter," "my beloved son," "my beloved child." To pray is to let that voice speak to the center of your being, to your guts, and let that voice resound in your whole being. Who am I? I am the beloved....[8]

Silence is both protection and correction. It shields us from the forces that rob our souls of dignity and purity, and it confronts the false messages that constantly flood our hearts. In their place it writes the truth of our identity and purpose. The messages of popular culture often conspire to tell us: "You are what you own. You are the sum of your wins and your losses. You are what you drive or wear." To this nonsense, God replies, "No, you are my beloved child, my chosen one. I knew you before you were born. I have eternal plans for you that will shine brightly when the last star goes dark." In his silent presence, the true picture of your self emerges like a brilliant photographic image in a darkroom. Silence and retreat are means to spiritual insight: "When you are disturbed, do not sin; ponder it on your beds, and be silent" (Psalm 4:4).

PRACTICAL MATTERS:
BRINGING THE DESERT HOME

There are things we can do to enter the quiet. Going on organized retreats where silence is a significant component is especially worthwhile. Fortunately, many retreat centers offer silent retreats, but work and family obligations limit these opportunities for many. Nevertheless, as Carlo Carretto has observed, if you cannot go to the desert, then the desert can come to you.

There are many ways to bring the desert home. Try "unplugging," that is, silencing those technological intruders (cell phones, iPods, pagers, computer games, laptops, TVs, etc.) for a period each day and each week. Consider setting time boundaries. (Starting small often does wonders.) Make an appointment with God (for quiet time, Scripture reading, meditation, etc.) and view the appointment as seriously as any appointment with a boss or a doctor. Likewise, try engaging in "little solitudes"—such as savoring your coffee quietly alone in the early morning hours before work, disappearing at lunch with a favorite book in hand, walking, or exercising. One of my favorites is choosing to live one hour a week without words. It is an exercise worth trying, as is engaging in a hobby that requires no speech. Any of these activities can make a surprising difference in our lives.

Another practice in which many find power is short, one-sentence prayers. These can be recited while waiting at the stop light or in the grocery line. The Jesus Prayer ("Jesus Christ, Son of God, have mercy on me, a sinner") or a single line from one of the Psalms stands ready to offer calm to a troubled heart. To facilitate this practice, every Christian should consider building a small library of prayer books, beginning with the Psalms (the first prayer book of believers) and the *Book of Common Prayer*.[9] In addition, the number of excellent books that treat silence, meditation, and prayer is large and growing. Reading Richard Foster, Marjorie Thompson, Dallas Willard and others will greatly enrich one's understanding and practice.[10]

Entering the quiet may work better if others join us on the journey. This may seem paradoxical (since solitude usually implies aloneness), but silence and solitude are more about a posture of the spirit than a head count. Silence in the company of others can be very moving, even life-changing. This may explain the current popularity of retreats in which silence is a key feature. Recall that when Jesus retreated, he often brought along his inner circle, Peter, James, and John. One may go to Gethsemane with close spiritual friends.

If practicing silence were easy, many Christians would have already made it a daily feature of their lives. The truth is, the practice is hard, a slight to our dignity, a painful self-effacement, a sacrifice. Nouwen warns:

> The trouble is, as soon as you sit and become quiet, you think, *Oh, I forgot this. I should call my friend. Later on I'm going to see him.* Your inner life is like a banana tree filled with monkeys jumping up and down. It's not easy to sit and trust that in solitude God will speak to you—not as a magical voice but that he will let you know something gradually over the years.[11]

MY EXPERIENCE OF SILENCE

Practicing silence is radically countercultural. It is certainly not something I can claim to have mastered. I grew up in a boisterous household of eight—six siblings and two parents. We talked, laughed, and argued a lot, and we still do. Mealtimes were sometimes as animated and noisy as the floor of the New York Stock Exchange. Discussions of politics or the smallest item in the daily news could lead to explosions of opinion with everyone talking at once. My mother often quoted the Groucho Marx line, "I was vaccinated with a phonograph needle" (so apparently were we all). Gatherings of the extended family were frequent, which meant our house overflowed with dozens of grandparents, aunts, uncles, and cousins, who were equally garrulous—often arguing and telling stories into the wee hours. In this overly excited, verbal world I thrived, but I also grew weary. I needed quiet and it came, though in ways I didn't particularly like.

First, there was the solitary farm work. We owned a farm about forty-five miles from our house. Some evenings and on many weekends during the school year, and for some stretches in the summers, my dad, brothers, and I would work on the farm.

In high school I also worked long hours for a German Mennonite farmer near town. Work on these farms was hard, not merely because of the physical labor and the long days, but because of the enforced isolation and the long silences. I spent some entire days in the field without hearing another human voice. The solitude deeply affected me as I grew to appreciate it. It became my time to imagine, dream, and pray.

Another kind of silence was my experience as a boy. I had big questions for God, questions about things I just didn't understand about my world or myself. I recall retreating to the backyard (my sanctuary away from the household clamor) to think and pray alone under the night stars. There I asked for answers, but what I received was silence. I asked again and again and still I received no satisfaction. I now believe, all these years later, that God was teaching me in the silences of the field and my backyard prayer life. He was giving me understanding and preparing me for service in ways I could not have imagined.

Even as a young man, I was beginning to learn that I was not in charge. I was being taught by the silence that listening is truly a form of faith, and faith requires resolve, routine, and humility. Not talking, not doing, not being in charge, not having all the answers—these things offended my dignity. Listening in the midst of silence seemed paradoxical: both too easy and unbearably hard. Only in adulthood could I begin to understand what was going on. Simone Weil shrewdly notes: "There is an easiness in salvation which is more difficult to us than all our efforts."[12]

Sooner or later, if we would be spiritually mature, we will find the patience to enter the quiet. Over time, we will see how different life looks once we take this journey. No longer frenzied and fearful, the pilgrim heart will find "a spring of water gushing up" within that never needs replenishing. It is the secret of spiritual renewal (John 4:14).

11

DISCERNING: THE GIFT OF WISDOM

Test the spirits to see whether they are from God.
1 John 4:1

Where is the wisdom we have lost in knowledge?
Where is the knowledge we have lost in information?
—T. S. Eliot

In August 1835 a twenty-two-year-old Søren Kierkegaard struggled to understand what he was to do with his life. In his private journal, like myriads of young adults before and after him, he poured out his anguished uncertainty:

What I really need is to be clear about *what I must do*, not what I must know....What matters is to find a purpose, to see what it really is that God wills that *I* should do; the crucial thing is to find a truth which is truth *for me*, to find *the idea for which I am willing to live and die*....[O]f what use would it be to me to be able to formulate the meaning of Christianity...if it had no deeper meaning *for me and for my life?*[1]

Having taught college students for more than thirty years, I have seen up close the uncertainty about life young Kierkegaard expressed. Yet it is not just twentysome-things who ask such basic questions. Who among us has not wondered what God really wishes us to do? What shall our life's work be? Whom shall we marry? Or shall we marry at all? To what cause shall we devote ourselves? How do we balance the many competing claims on our lives, our time, our duties, our resources? How will we ever know for sure the path we should take?

Nothing is more important than understanding one's purpose in life—what might more properly be called one's *vocation*, in the original sense of hearing and obeying God's call. Yet few concepts are as murky or capable of distortion as "calling." This has been so for quite a long time. In the sixteenth century William Shakespeare gently mocked the Puritans (who loved to talk about vocation) through his portrayal of the rotund, beer-swilling Falstaff. When Prince Hal accused Falstaff of purse snatching, Falstaff's defense is theological, "Why, Hal, 'tis my vocation, Hal. 'Tis no sin for a man to labor in his vocation."[2]

Most people would not so brazenly justify their vices as God's calling, yet some do it every day. Consider, for example, terrorists who kill "infidels" because it is their divine mandate. There is always a danger lurking that our personal preferences and prejudices will turn out—coincidentally—to look exactly like the will of God. I see a growing temptation among some Christians today to call whatever happens "God's will," so long as it is personally favorable to them. Is every good outcome (at least what appears to be a good outcome) necessarily a "God thing"? If so, what do we call the bad things that happen to us or others? Person A puts his house on the market, and "miraculously" it sells in three days. Person B puts his house on the market, and it lingers there untouched for twelve months. Person A, if he is pious, may very well declare his success God's will. But we have to ask: What if Person B is equally devoted and pious, but his house doesn't sell? What then? Is his bad luck also God's will? Whose will is it when things go very badly despite our most fervent prayers and wishes? How, we might ask, do we avoid the self-serving distortion in which we baptize our own preferences and declare them "the will of God"?

The answer is spiritual discernment, which is both a skill to be developed and the product of spiritual transformation. The Apostle had this in mind when he wrote: "Do not be conformed to this world, but be transformed by the renewing of your minds, *so that you may discern what is the will of God*—what is good and acceptable and perfect" (Romans 12:2, my emphasis). The capacity to discern the good, the acceptable, and the perfect is not unlike other spiritual disciplines that are passionately sought, deliberately cultivated, and freely received as divine blessings.

Daily we come to forks in the road, and we must choose. Even if we sincerely and earnestly want to choose "the road less traveled," we sometimes have trouble knowing which path to take. Robert Frost describes this dilemma of choosing in his well-known poem "The Road Not Taken":

> Two roads diverged in a yellow wood,
>
> And sorry I could not travel both
>
> And be one traveler, long I stood
>
> And looked down one as far as I could
>
> To where it bent in the undergrowth....

As the narrator goes on to explain, there was no obvious reason to choose one path rather than the other, for "both [roads] that morning *equally* lay / In leaves that no step had trodden black" (my emphasis).The point is that, at the critical moment when the choice had to be made, the narrator could not easily distinguish one path from the other, for they were worn "really about the same." Though the narrator did finally choose, he admits his uncertainty. The route he took had "*perhaps* the better claim" (my emphasis), he says. Frost's dilemma represents what happens to us all. Our toughest decisions do not concern the clear choices between good and bad, right and wrong. Rather we are faced with negotiating in the fog, when the options and the consequences of our choices are far from obvious. We long for clarity like the many students I have listened to over the years, as they anguish over their choices. Fortunately, Scripture offers excellent guidance.

THE GIFT TO BE RECEIVED

Discernment begins with prayer. When Solomon faced the daunting prospect of leading a nation, he asked for wisdom: "Give your servant therefore an understanding mind to govern your people, able to discern between good and evil; for who can govern this your great people?" (1 Kings 3:9). The Lord's reply is positive: "I now do according to your word. Indeed I give you a wise and discerning mind; no one like you has been before you and no one like you shall arise after you" (3:12). In the New Testament, James offers similar counsel: "If any of you is lacking in wisdom,

ask God, who gives to all generously and ungrudgingly, and it will be given you"
(James 1:5). While there is much we can do to acquire a discerning heart (discussed
in the remainder of this chapter), we must keep in mind that discernment is first a
spiritual gift (1 Corinthians 2:15; 12:10). In the words of Parker Palmer, discernment
is more a gift to be received than a goal to be achieved.[3] It is a gracious benefit to be
welcomed, cultivated, and exercised.

LOVING AND LIVING THE WORD

The novelist Salman Rushdie delivered a speech in 2005 on the extraordinary
power of great books. Though he was commenting on secular writing, what he said,
with slight adjustment, applies to Scripture. He noted that when we truly love a
good book, it changes us:

> [L]ove gets under one's guard and shakes things up, for such is its sneaky
> nature. When a reader falls in love with a book, it leaves its essence inside
> him, like radioactive fallout on an arable field, and after that there are
> certain crops that will no longer grow in him, while other, stranger, more
> fantastic growths may occasionally be produced. We love relatively few
> books in our lives, and those books become parts of the way we see our
> lives; we read our lives through them, and their descriptions of the inner
> and outer worlds become mixed up with ours—they become ours.[4]

This, of course, is a description of the power of Scripture when we listen to it faithfully
and lovingly. We "read our lives" through the stories, precepts, and examples found in
God's word. The world of Scripture becomes "mixed up with" our lives, providing us
wisdom and insight for daily decisions. More than that, the Bible gives us a basis for
action, a template, a "manual" for performance: "The word is very near you; it is in your
mouth and in your heart, so that you can do it" (Deuteronomy 30:14, RSV). Scripture is
the basis "for every good work," Paul tells Timothy, "useful for teaching, for reproof, for
correction, and for training in righteousness" (2 Timothy 3:16-17). To a great
degree, discernment comes through immersion in Scripture.[5]

Yet Scriptural meaning is not always self-evident. The Bible does not read itself.
The only people who read it are human beings; and, being fallible, they need help.

The Ethiopian eunuch, an untutored seeker, speaks for us all when he asks, "How can I [understand the Bible], unless someone guides me?" (Acts 8:31). Scripture is best understood when we read it humbly within the community of the faithful. Gregory the Great noted: "While there were many things in the sacred word that I could not come to understand by myself, I could often grasp their sense when I was in the presence of the brothers."[6] To incorporate Scriptural teaching into one's life, a great deal is demanded of us—first and foremost deep love for God and his word, but also humility and a spirit of openness. According to Paul, "knowledge and full insight" derive from a life overflowing with love (Philippians 1:9-10). The trinity of love, knowledge, and insight then empower one "to determine what is best."

Agape love seems to be both the means to Scriptural insight, as well as its fruitful outcome. In other words, we cannot separate who we are as persons from how we read, understand, or reflect. Ethics (how we behave) and hermeneutics (how we interpret) are necessarily linked.[7] A wonderful case in point can be seen in Gerard Manley Hopkins's reply to his friend Robert Bridges, when Bridges wrote to Hopkins, a new convert, asking how he might also come to believe in Christ. Hopkins answered simply, "Give alms." Flannery O'Connor once commented on Hopkins's advice to his friend: "[Hopkins] was trying to say to Bridges that God is to be experienced in Charity (in the sense of love for the divine image in human beings). Don't get so entangled with intellectual difficulties that you fail to look for God in this way."[8] Love or charity is not only the outcome of a proper reading of the Bible; love is also the source of better interpretations, clear thinking, and right action. Love is superior to knowledge or hermeneutical prowess: "Knowledge puffs up, but love builds up" (1 Corinthians 8:1).

WWJT—WHAT WOULD JESUS THINK?

Discernment is the product of careful thinking. Spiritual understanding comes through prayer flowing from a loving heart, but not necessarily through prayer and love alone. As Professor Douglas Groothius has argued, Jesus was "a disciplined and discriminating intellect." His "teachings, debates, and even prayers indicate a logical mind at work. The Gospels document Jesus pronouncing divine judgment on occasion, but not at the expense of reason, evidence, and analysis."[9] The follower of Jesus, then, understands the importance of gathering information, listening carefully, and evaluating patiently. Indeed, many of the virtues of the good scholar (e.g., humility, honesty, patience, creativity, etc.) are also virtues of the follower of Jesus. Paul tells the disciples in Corinth to "weigh what is said" (1 Corinthians 14:29). The Hebrew writer defines the mature person as one who has been "trained *by practice* to distinguish good from evil" (Hebrews 5:14, my emphasis). Using one's mind to make distinctions is a basic goal of every mature person. The Bible calls this "testing the spirits" (1 John 4:1).

We live at a time when rationality is often denigrated. "Listen to your heart, the voice within," is the popular mantra. And there is, indeed, wisdom in one's heart, properly understood.[10] "The last act of reason is to recognize that there are an infinite number of things that are beyond its grasp....The heart has its reasons, which the reason does not know....We know the truth, not only through reason, but also through the heart," Pascal says.[11] But to recognize the limits of reason is very different from dismissing or ignoring reason. To ignore reason is to court disaster. Ideally, reason and the heart work together. Pascal, the great seventeenth-century scientist, recognized that the language of reason and the language of the heart are the warp and woof of an integrated life. Indeed, he showed that the goal is to think with one's heart, one's head, and one's imagination. Together they yield stunning insight.

HUMILITY IN INSIGHT

I have already argued that humility is a feature of good intellectual work, but this virtue is so central to discernment that it deserves special attention. Yale psychologist Robert Sternberg edited an insightful book concerning human behavior entitled *Why Smart People Can Be So Stupid*.[12] Sternberg points out that very intelligent people (as measured by high IQs) are remarkably susceptible to unintelligent behavior, including, one supposes, standing at the crossroad, pondering long and hard, then taking the wrong road. Why is this, he wondered? After much research, Dr. Sternberg concluded that intelligence, if it is not attached to certain moral virtues, can lead to dreadful behavior. (Many criminals, for example, have high IQs.)

Intellectually gifted people commonly overestimate their powers. Because they are smart in one domain, they assume that they are clever in areas beyond their expertise. Their arrogance becomes their downfall.

Fundamental to Sternberg's thesis is the distinction between knowledge and wisdom. T. S. Eliot asks:

Where is the wisdom we have lost in knowledge?

Where is the knowledge we have lost in information?"[13]

Sternberg observes that while IQ scores are rising about nine points per generation, people are not necessarily becoming wiser. Intelligence simply cannot be equated with wisdom, which entails qualities like compassion, honesty, and reciprocity, and the "golden rule" (charity towards all).

Discernment requires humility, in particular. The Christian tradition warns steadfastly against the blinding force of pride: "God opposes the proud, but gives grace to the humble....Humble yourselves before the Lord, and he will exalt you" (James 4:6, 10). Thomas à Kempis advises, "All men are frail, but thou shouldst reckon none as frail as thyself." The idea is central to Pascal too. People who understand best are "those who have a humble heart and who love lowliness, whatever kind of mind they may have, lofty or low."[14] A constant awareness of our own frailty, vulnerability, and tendency to error can protect us against our worst decisions.

WISDOM IN COMMUNITY

Discernment is most often discovered in community. Just as Timothy listened to Paul, everyone needs spiritual guides and mentors. Wise leaders, flesh-and-blood voices long experienced in wisdom, often are the best source of counsel; hence, the place of "elders" and spiritual fathers and mothers in both the ancient Jewish synagogue and in the early Christian congregation. When one stands at the crossroad looking for direction, one should ask: *Who are my companions on the journey? Who challenges my thinking? Who interrogates and exposes my hidden motives, my pride, my blind spots, my selfish desires? Who keeps me honest? To whom am I listening with utmost attention?* Unfortunately, not everyone who presents himself or herself as a spiritual leader is wise. One of the great misfortunes of any Christian community is the presence of leaders who do not exhibit the cardinal Christian virtues in abundance. We should listen to those who show clear evidence of maturity, for which there are external measures, i.e., the fruit of the Spirit—love, joy, peace, patience, kindness, generosity, faithfulness, gentleness, and self-control (Galatians 5:22). We must beware of those who may wear titles but who lack the fruit of the Spirit.

Decisions affecting others, especially the congregational life, ought to be particularly subject to communal scrutiny.[15] The Jerusalem Council provides one remarkable example of how the ancient church took concrete steps to make certain that a divisive issue was settled communally. "The apostles and the elders met together to consider this matter" (Acts 15:6). "The whole assembly kept silence, and listened to Barnabas and Paul...." (v. 12). James added further testimony, citing Old Testament passages to support the position argued by Barnabas and Paul (vv. 13-17). "Then the apostles and the elders, *with the consent of the whole church,* decided..." (v. 22, my emphasis). Throughout the New Testament, one sign of a good decision is that it encourages "the common good" and builds up the body (1 Corinthians 12:7; Ephesians 4:12). Like all spiritual gifts, discernment is not intended primarily for personal benefit but for the good of the community.

DISCERNMENT AND "DOWNWARD MOBILITY"

Discernment may require "downward mobility." Once more, we return to the theme of *kenosis*. As the pilgrim heart seeks to determine God's will, it must be wary of the inauthentic call, the one that may satisfy only personal preferences, flatter the ego, or promise personal gain. Bonhoeffer reminds us: "When Christ calls a man, he bids him come and die." True discipleship is costly—both to pocketbook and ego. Jesus' way leads downward, to the place of the poor, the marginalized, and the dispossessed. Nouwen confesses in *The Road to Daybreak*: "Everything in me wants to move upward. Downward mobility with Jesus goes radically against my inclinations, against the advice of the world surrounding me, and against the culture of which I am a part."[16] While there can and should be great joy in seeking one's calling, one must be on guard when one's apparent call turns out to be a mere expression of the American Dream—the promise of more money, more prestige, and more creature comforts.

In the end, discernment demands great doses of self-reflection and the renunciation of anything that comes between us and the will of God. Suzanne Farnham and her colleagues suggest a number of things ("idols") that may come between us and God's will. These include our own cultural values (our love of success, individualism, self-sufficiency, etc.), desire for prosperity, self-interest, desire for security, and self-doubt.[17] Perhaps it is here that we face the greatest seduction of all, for it can be hard to distinguish our deepest desires from the divine will. While our preferences and God's will may be in agreement, we must be cautious in saying so. We must "test the spirits" to be sure, and this includes rigorously applying all the criteria of discernment available to us. If we are not open to the possibility of enjoying less security, less wealth, and less prestige—if, in other words, we are not open to "poverty of spirit"—then we may greatly hinder our capacity to recognize the true will of God.

UNCERTAINTY AND "THE INWARD POINT OF POISE"

Warning: True discernment does not guarantee certainty. Many assume that if they receive a clear "call" from God, then they will be protected from doubt or failure. Everyone wants certainty, of course. In an age of self-help manuals, Oprah, and Dr. Phil, quick fixes and sure-fire formulas have a strong allure; but spiritual maturity means living with a certain level of uncertainty and an honest awareness of our own suspect motives. Walking by faith means that we do not enjoy full sight or absolute certainty.[18] We "trust and obey" as we peer through a glass darkly. Trust implies risk and—in the short term—even apparent failure.

As I hear people—especially young adults—weigh their futures, I sometimes envision a giant road map. It is as though they view their lives as a great journey across the continent. They are starting out in New York, and they must reach San Francisco. The trouble is, as they stare at the road map, they become bewildered by the array of routes—there are the main interstates, the federal highways, and an overwhelming number of lesser "blue highways." These young adults sometimes despair because they suppose that God has preordained only one particular way for them; but, given the number of options, they cannot seem to find that One True Path.

Such a view of life inspires anxiety, yet nothing in Scripture says that God dictates such particularity for our lives—at least not as a rule. Could it be that one's real duty is not to find the one true highway, but rather to be a certain kind of person—humble, attentive, and obedient—whatever the path one is on? If "The Way" be in us, John Bunyan once said, then we will always be in The Way, wherever we travel. Kierkegaard seems to have come to the same conclusion. It's not our latitude and longitude that count, but being close to God and finding "the inward point of poise," as he called it.[19]

Uncertainty and pain do not necessarily signal a mistake. Even when we are on the right path, doubt may find us. Consider John the Baptist. Alone in prison and facing execution, John began to doubt whether he had been called to be the great announcer of the Messiah: "Are you he who is to come, or shall we look for another?" he asked (Luke 7:19). The prophet not only experienced doubt about Jesus—the very one he had baptized and upon whom the Spirit had descended in the form of the dove—John also experienced self-doubt. One can do exactly the right thing with one's life, like John, yet experience consternation. Faithfulness means being patient, attentive, and constant, even in the dark places. It does not mean freedom from doubt.

THE LONG VIEW

But what if we really do take the wrong turn? What then? As many stories in the Bible demonstrate, discernment demands the long view. Human time-frames are simply too tiny to reveal the full story. We paint in miniature, but God's canvas is greater than the cosmos itself. Our brief scene unfolds in minutes, while God's master plot fills eternity. We must stretch to see how our little stories fit into his grand narrative. Biblically speaking, our story began before we were born, even before the world was fashioned. Paul illustrates the hope that arises when you see the full panorama:

> Long before [God] laid down earth's foundations, he had us in mind, had settled on us as the focus of his love, to be made whole and holy by his love. Long, long ago he decided to adopt us into his family through Jesus Christ.

(What pleasure he took in planning this!) He wanted us to enter into the celebration of his lavish gift-giving by the hand of his beloved Son....Long before we first heard of Christ and got our hopes up, he had his eye on us, had designs on us for glorious living, part of the overall purpose he is working in everything and everyone. (Ephesians 1, *The Message*)

We understand that a child is the "product" of the parents' genetics. Similarly, we know that a child may be shaped by the moral choices of parents, grandparents, and others—even if these choices were made before the child's birth, and even if the child remains ignorant of them. In a similar way, the Bible asserts that our true identity derives from our long spiritual history which began ages ago. We begin not with a blank slate, but with a divine agenda, implanted by our Creator. We find our purpose, therefore, when we understand our spiritual origin. Because we are created in God's image, because we derive from him and will return to him, we possess an immutable identity, as distinct as our fingerprints or our DNA. And the key is this: *our identity encodes our vocation and our mission.*

Just as our purpose was established eons ago, our vocation continues even after we die, for our actions today will outlast this mortal life. Given this breathtaking span, it becomes problematic to try to measure the value of a life close at hand. Who has the empirical instrument to measure something that transcends space and time? To grasp this point we might think of how some professions are appreciated for their important multi-generational effects. Painting, architecture, ministry, child-care, and teaching are among them. Henry Adams correctly observed: "A teacher affects eternity; he can never tell where his influence stops."

In a similar fashion every life has the potential to touch lives beyond its own. Each day we stir invisible ripples in the pool of life that will arc through eternity. A few, such as Otto Schindler, do this in dramatic ways. Schindler's courageous defiance of the Nazis in World War II resulted in thousands of people, the descendants of those on his "list," living today. Many others—quietly, humbly and invisibly—perform simple deeds each day that also yield fruit for eternity. Jesus tells us that the farmer plants seeds, and they will grow and produce great fruit, though the farmer does not know how (Mark 4:26-27). That's a picture of human life in miniature. Discernment means living by faith, which also means refusing to let clocks, calendars, salaries, or sales reports determine the worth of a life.

THE GRACE OF DISCERNMENT

It's worth remembering that wisdom is not for sale. No university offers a degree in sagacity. Understanding the will of God—ultimate wisdom, in other words—is not the product of a formula or a course of study. Rather, it is the fruit of a comprehensive way of life that God makes possible. It is the gift of a gracious God, who gives to those who ask.[20] But it should be noticed that he gives to those who posture themselves in a way to receive. The one who listens in humble submission; who gathers and weighs the available information; who meditates and waits; who immerses himself or herself in Scripture; who befriends wise leaders and spiritual guides; who studies the "big picture" of salvation history; who receives the collective wisdom of the church and its leaders; and who welcomes the indwelling presence of the Holy Spirit—this is the one most likely to attain "the mind of Christ" (1 Corinthians 2:16).

12

SINGING: THE WAY TO HEAVEN'S DOOR

Be filled with the spirit, as you sing psalms and hymns
and spiritual songs among yourselves, singing and
making melody in your hearts....
Ephesians 5:18-19

Next to the Word of God, music deserves the highest praise.
—Martin Luther

In her highly original autobiography, *Traveling Mercies,* Anne Lamott tells the story of how she came to faith. In a period of despair, when she spent long, lonely days in a fog of alcohol, speed, and cocaine, spiraling towards destruction, something utterly unexpected occurred. During this dark time she visited a flea market in Marin City, California; and there she passed by a small, sad, ramshackle church from which she heard the most remarkable music. She called it "glorious noise." At the time, Lamott was hostile to Christianity. She could not bear to hear a sermon, but the music drew her in, and she returned for more in the following weeks. The singing, she said,

> was furry and resonant, coming from everyone's very heart. There was no
> sense of performance or judgment, only that the music was breath and food.
> Something inside me that was stiff and rotting would feel soft and tender.
> Somehow the singing wore down all the boundaries and distinctions that
> kept me so isolated. Sitting there, standing with them to sing, sometimes so

shaky and sick that I felt like I might tip over, I felt bigger than myself, like I
was being taken care of, tricked into coming back to life.[1]

One Sunday in April, 1984, Lamott attended the church again. She stayed for the
sermon that day, which she found unimpressive, but the music was mesmerizing:

The last song was so deep and raw and pure that I could not escape. It was
as if the people were singing in between the notes, weeping and joyful at
the same time, and I felt like their voices or something was rocking me in
its bosom, holding me like a scared kid, and I opened up to that feeling—
and it washed over me.[2]

According to Lamott, "it was the music that pulled me in and split me wide open."[3]
That day she decided she would become a Christian.

It would be hard to find a story that more vividly illustrates the power of music
to enthrall and move a person to action. Through the centuries, music has been a
primary means of conversion and spiritual formation, and it is happening today in
a surprising way.[4] For most believers, music is not a frill or an ornament, not some
illustration of a theological truth; much more, music is the good news in word and
sound, the purest and most potent expression of God's presence and transcendence,
and the best way to engage our hearts and imaginations, our bodies and souls.

If one studies the lives of great Christians through the centuries, the central place
of church music becomes clear. Augustine of Hippo is a case in point. The young
Augustine had an experience similar to Anne Lamott's. The church in Milan, under
the leadership of Ambrose, was famous as a center of fervent hymn singing, and the
music played a major role in Augustine's decision to become a disciple. Addressing
God in his *Confessions*, the great theologian writes:

How I wept during your hymns and songs! I was deeply moved by the music
of the sweet chants of your Church. The sounds flowed into my ears and the
truth was distilled into my heart. This caused the feelings of devotion to
overflow. Tears ran, and it was good for me to have that experience.[5]

What was true for Lamott and Augustine is true for many today. Anyone serious
about spiritual formation will give considerable attention to sacred music—the
music of congregational worship, the music of youth groups and youth gatherings,

and the music that fills our homes and automobiles. Kathleen Norris observes that when she was a child she thought "singing was the purpose of religion."[6] If singing is not the purpose of religion, it is most certainly one of its principal supports.

THE BREATH OF GOD'S PRESENCE

People are influenced by music because it has the power to transport them into God's presence. It can awaken them to dimensions beyond their ordinary experience and kindle in them a love for God's majesty, power, and splendor. Though this can also happen in prayer, Scripture reading, or a sermon, for most people it happens in music. It leads us into sacred space, sacred time. According to George Herbert, England's greatest devotional poet and an accomplished musician, church music is "the way to heaven's door."[7] Contemporary composers, worship leaders, and theologians make similar points. "Worship thrives on wonder," explains Matt Redman, who, with his wife Beth, authored the popular contemporary hymn "Blessed Be Your Name":

> We can admire, appreciate, and perhaps even adore someone without a
> sense of wonder. But we cannot worship without wonder. For worship to
> be worship, it must contain something of the otherness of God....[God] is
> altogether glorious—unequalled in splendor and unrivalled in power. He
> is beyond the grasp of human reason—far above the reach of even the
> loftiest scientific mind. Inexhaustible, immeasurable and unfathomable—
> eternal, immortal and invisible.[8]

Music, more than any other aspect of worship, has the capacity to awaken us to this sense of God's otherness.

Christian hymns invite us to delight in God's presence, not merely think about him. Music awakens us to God's matchless power, beauty, and transcendence—his sheer otherness. Music can simultaneously make us feel God's grandeur and our smallness compared to him. This is why, whenever a worshiper approaches God—as seen in Isaiah 6:1-5 or throughout the Book of Revelation—the worshiper invariably resorts to symbolic language, image, and song to describe the uncanny experience. These are the "tools" of the worshiper to suggest the unsearchable, ineffable nature of God. "O the depth of the riches and wisdom and knowledge of God!" (Romans 11:33).

Without music we are left with talk. The trouble with talk is that it tends to position the speaker in a place of power. It puts one in charge, which can border on a dangerous conceit when it comes to reporting on the Almighty. A different, humbler posture of spirit emerges in worship and song. When we are singing, there is a sense that we are not in charge. The leading comes from the music—or it should. Anne Lamott's experience illustrates how we may submit to the power of the song (and therefore to the Reality behind the music): "I felt like their voices or something was rocking me in its bosom, holding me like a scared kid, and I opened up to that feeling—and it washed over me." Music has this power to hold us, open us up, and bathe us. It happens *to* us. And when it is taken seriously—when it involves a whole-body immersion—it brings us to God.

For those suspicious of emotion, music's power to take us where the intellect cannot go is alarming, but Scriptural example should allay our fears. The very fact that the Bible contains hundreds of song texts, many highly emotional in nature, tells us something important. Consider Mary's song of praise (Luke 1:46-55). It expresses more than doctrinal truths (though it does that). The song overflows in ecstasy as the Virgin realizes she is to bear the Christ child. If we do not feel Mary's transport, if we do not sense the sheer surprise and wonder pulsating in her words of praise, then we are deaf to the glorious music in the text.

In similar fashion the great songs of the Old Testament (especially the Psalms) express strong emotion—exultant joy like Mary's, but also deep sorrow, brittle anxiety, raw fear, and luminous hope. The whole range of human emotion is captured in the Psalms, and this is precisely why we need them in our communal and private worship. The Psalms permit us, indeed require us, to be fully human before our fellow worshipers and before God. They dissolve our pretensions to having it "all together." They expose our "niceness" as the sham that it is. They demand truth from us—not just pretty thoughts in our heads, but the full conviction and the passion of our hearts. Surely, if all the Psalms (not just a few favorites) were restored to the worship of the church, we would be a more authentic and faithful community.[9]

Singing succeeds because—like other spiritual practices—it requires the full involvement of the whole person. There is no other act of worship that is so visceral. This is especially so of congregational singing, for every voice is fully required. Those who have been reared within an *a cappella* tradition may have trouble understanding its peculiar beauty and uniqueness. A few years ago I attended a service at the Kazan Cathedral in St. Petersburg, Russia. The music, as is true of most Orthodox worship, was *a cappella*. Those voices, singing melodies and harmonies in a tongue strange to me, were exquisitely touching, rapturous in their purity. On another occasion a woman in a Catholic Church in Oregon describes an experience analogous to mine:

> After the entire assembly had gone forward, received Holy Communion, and returned to their pew, a second communion song was sung a cappella. Having that happen at the time of Holy Communion when we had just received our Lord's sacramental presence really just tied together what we had done, what we had moved to, what we were all experiencing, and what we were then singing.[10]

Singing has always been the church's means to teach, inspire, and build community. On the night Jesus was betrayed, he sang hymns with his followers (Matthew 26:30; Mark 14:26). Doxologies, hymn fragments, and references to congregational singing run through Paul's letters.[11] The Apostle urges Christians to employ song to teach, praise God, encourage one another, and express thanks:

> Let the word of Christ dwell in you richly; teach and admonish one another in all wisdom; and with gratitude in your hearts sing psalms, hymns, and spiritual songs to God....[S]ing psalms and hymns and spiritual songs among yourselves, singing and making melody in your hearts....
> (Colossians 3:16; Ephesians 5:19)

Singing builds community like nothing else, as Don Saliers points out:

> In our present North American cultural context, the singing assemblies in our churches...are among the very few remaining places where words and music actually form human beings into a communal identity....[W]hen people meet to worship, public singing still offers formation in a shared

identity. This identity flows out of an ancient story that continues to take on new life, in words and tunes that speak today. It gives voice to individual people in praise, lament, and need, but it does not leave them isolated, surrounding them instead with a great choir.[12]

EMOTION, INSTRUCTION, ACTION

Music moves us in more ways than one. Not only does it stir our emotions; it can also prompt us to make life-altering decisions (as in the case of Augustine and Lamott). The force of hymns is often extraordinary because, when we sing, body, emotion, and intellect are mysteriously connected. Great Christian hymns are effective because they implant the truths of the faith in our hearts, not just in our heads. They rehearse the stories of Scripture. In word and sound we experience Gethsemane, the cross, and the resurrection. We remember our sinfulness, our need for redemption, our duty to our neighbor, and the promise of eternal life. In a time when people have a diminished capacity to absorb long sermons, hymns stand ready to offer important inspirational and didactic service to the church, as they have done for millennia. It's worth noting that the first piece of written English (of which we have a record) is a hymn. English literary history began when, in the seventh century, an Anglo-Saxon songwriter named Caedman composed a hymn telling the story of creation, which was used to bring pagans to faith.

Given the power of song to shape belief and move people to action, we should pay close attention to content. That which we sing, we tend to believe.[13] This can be a very good thing. In a theologically shallow environment, singing may redeem an otherwise impoverished service. As a youth I heard sermons that occasionally tended towards legalism or moralism, yet the service was full of songs like "Amazing Grace," "A Wonderful Savior," and "Love Lifted Me." The sermon may have been ensnared in law, but the music was rich in grace. In the same way, sometimes I heard sermons that warned against the dangers of excessive religious fervor, but then the congregation would stand and fervently sing:

When each can feel his brother's sigh,

And with him bear a part;

> When sorrow flows from eye to eye,
>
> And joy from heart to heart.

William Bradbury's stirring music and Joseph Swain's touching lyrics trumped the sermon of the day, for what we sing and feel in our hearts remains with us far longer than what we receive through passive listening.[14] So it has always been, for hymns are "active theology."[15] According to Don E. Saliers, "the continuing worship of God in the assembly is a form of theology. In fact it is 'primary theology.' Worship... is a theological act."[16]

Paul understood the capacity of hymns to impart core spiritual truths. When he wished to encourage Christians to live sacrificial lives, he didn't limit his discourse to reasoned argument. Instead, he appealed to people's memory of worship, citing a familiar hymn, the great "Carmen Christi" or Song of Christ (Philippians 2:5-11). On other occasions the great missionary-evangelist quoted poetry or hymns to illustrate his message and move his readers or listeners to act (Ephesians 5:14; 1 Timothy 3:16; Acts 17:28).

COMFORT AND COMMUNITY

Singing is vitally important to spirituality because it builds community. We have seen how Anne Lamott found consolation and community in the music. When the church in ancient Milan suffered persecution, Augustine reports that Ambrose's hymns provided encouragement and hope to the oppressed believers. The fact is that when a congregation sings "Be Still My Soul," "Listen to Our Hearts," or "When Peace Like a River," it is mysteriously consoled and nourished in the same way spirituals comforted oppressed African-Americans in the days of slavery. James Baldwin expresses the power of gospel music in an old-fashioned revival:

> As the singing filled the air the watching, listening faces underwent a change, the eyes focusing on something within; the music seemed to soothe a poison out of them; and time seemed nearly to fall away from the sullen, belligerent, battered faces, as though they were fleeing back to their first condition, while dreaming of their last.[17]

Sacred song tells our story and, somehow, makes it all right. In the music we recite "the tale of how we suffer, and how we are delighted, and how we may triumph...."[18]

Music is vital to faith because it is a primary aid to memory. Hearing a song from our childhood can instantly catapult us to a precise location and moment—when we were singing in church, on a mission trip, on a retreat, or in the school choir. This mnemonic power is all to the good because spirituality presupposes, indeed demands, vivid recollection.

Of course, music's power is not limited to church settings. In one of the lowest moments of my life, I recall how the music from a particular movie deeply ministered to my broken spirit. The 1986 film *The Mission* contains some of the most memorable music in film history. Ennio Morricone's score greatly amplifies the story of eighteenth-century missionaries to the Guarani Indians of South America. Through panpipes, drums, unusual rhythms, and hymn-like chanting, Morricone conveys a story of sin, suffering love, tragic sacrifice, and redemption. During a time of particular stress I recall listening to this score over and over, sensing the undercurrents of pain, pathos, and devotion in the melodies. I drew strength and courage from this music, as it seemed to invite me to be strong, hold on, and be faithful. From Morricone I could see that even "secular" music can serve a spiritual purpose. I have friends who report the same power in classical, jazz or contemporary Christian music. All sorts of music can minister to us in all sorts of ways.

PROBLEMS AND SOLUTIONS:
HUMILITY AND FLEXIBILITY

Precisely because music is so important, we should not be surprised that anxiety is often aroused when a congregation contemplates changes in its worship. As we sort through the changes, everyone concerned needs an extra measure of patience and humility. The array of styles of church music is vast, yet most of us have been exposed to only a very limited spectrum. Thousands of hymns have been written over the last two thousand years, and only a few of these are known to us. If we turn to the Bible for guidance, we find that it never prescribes musical styles or particular hymns. Styles change, and no single era has an exclusive claim on musical excellence.

Every age has its forgettable tunes and inadequate lyrics as well as its masterpieces, but even the mediocre ones may be vehicles of faith for some.

It is worth remembering that "[t]he meaning of music resides in people, not in sounds."[19] So, one's personal judgment of a song's worth may be quite off the mark. I recall traveling for a week through Israel, hearing Middle Eastern music emanating from automobiles, restaurants, and homes as we drove through Arabic, Jewish and Druze neighborhoods. Was the music good or bad? I simply had no context to judge. Given everyone's limited experience of music, and given the extraordinary breadth of music available today—classical and contemporary, local and international, European and Eastern, Catholic and Protestant, mainstream and charismatic renewal—being slow to judge the worth of an unfamiliar musical form is the charitable way.

Should we try to raise the general quality of music in worship? Yes, certainly. Excellence in music, as in all things, is a desirable goal. If music is as remotely important in spiritual formation as I am claiming, then training excellent music leaders makes sense. Perhaps the day is not far off when congregations will devote as much attention to worship music as they do to the preaching or youth programs. How much better would our worship be if we asked a few basic questions like these:

1. Are the people taught? (Are the music texts theologically true? Is the language comprehensible and meaningful?)
2. Are the people inspired? (Does the music engage the emotions?)
3. Do the people receive balance? (Is dignity balanced by exuberance? Is joy coupled with reverence?)
4. Are the people joined in a sense of community? (Does the music encourage participation by the full assembly?)
5. Is there a sense of awe? (Would a visitor exclaim, based upon the conduct of the service, "God is really among you"? 1 Corinthians 14:25)

Even if we don't achieve all these goals, even if our services lack something (as they will), spiritual formation in worship is possible, if the worship is practiced with sincerity and grounded in Scripture. Sophistication is not the goal. Passionate engagement is.

"THE WILD, HEROIC RIDE TO HEAVEN"

It is possible that the quest for the ideal hymn perfectly performed could obscure the goal of meeting God in worship. George Ives was a church musician and the father of the great American composer Charles Ives. The father taught his son to respect the power of vernacular music. Concerning a stone-mason who sang irritatingly off key, the father instructed Charles:

> Watch him closely and reverently, look into his face and hear the music of the ages. Don't pay too much attention to the sounds—for if you do, you may miss the music. You won't get a wild, heroic ride to heaven on pretty little sounds.[20]

George Ives's counsel is, perhaps unintentionally, a fine commentary on Ephesians 5:19. The singing that pleases God is the melody in the heart, not the tune on one's lips.

In the so-called "worship wars" too many people, trapped in futile debates about the "pretty little sounds," have sadly missed "the wild, heroic ride to heaven." If we would be but more patient and flexible, recognizing that our singing is our gift to God (and therefore not primarily about our tastes or what we like), then it would matter less whether the song selection matches our personal preferences. Christian music is first and foremost a simultaneous offering of our voices to God, a receiving of God's word to us, and a statement of our faith proffered to the world. If we must err in one direction, a missional attitude is prudent. In the spirit of Luther we should advocate music that wins the hearts of the young and the untaught. Robert Wuthnow has noted that when children are exposed to religious music, they are more likely to take religion and spirituality seriously when they become adults.[21] This being so, we should remember the youthful Augustines and the troubled Anne Lamotts lingering in our doorways, waiting to be touched by the good news of God.

MUSIC, "QUEEN OF THE SENSES"

Music may well be the most overlooked of all the spiritual practices. As I reflect upon my own spiritual journey, I realize that music has been teacher, encourager, and friend. I vividly recall the day in high school when I decided that I wanted to attend a Christian college, a decision that forever changed the direction of my life. That same day a college choir was performing in a church not far from where I lived, and a group from my church attended the evening services and the concert that followed. As the choir strode solemnly into the sanctuary, singing a hauntingly beautiful hymn, my heart melted. The music "dissolve[d] me into ecstasies" and brought "all Heav'n before mine eyes," as Milton expressed it.[22] Though I can't recall the specific hymns sung that evening, the effect of that music remains with me to this day. I am no great singer, but that doesn't matter. I knew that evening that I wanted to be in a place where such music is possible. Words of faith set to music convert us, encourage us, console us, sustain us, and take us to heaven's door. There would be little discipleship or spiritual formation without songs, hymns, and spiritual songs.

13

CREATING: THE TRUTH OF BEAUTY

God is beautiful. He is the most beautiful of beings....
He is beautiful through Himself and in Himself, beautiful absolutely.
—Jacques Maritain

One thing I asked of the Lord, that will I seek after: to live in the house
of the Lord all the days of my life, to behold the beauty of the Lord,
and to inquire in his temple.
Psalm 27:4

Followers of Jesus face a dilemma. On the one hand, like all human beings, they find great pleasure in the glories of nature and in the beautiful things made by human hands. However, if life with God is our ultimate destination, could it be that all the beautiful things around us are really dangerous distractions? Might beauty be a perilous net, a mortal trap, for the heart bound for the Promised Land? Through the centuries Christians have been quite divided on such questions.

Some have strongly warned against the subtle dangers of beauty. The very sensuousness of the arts and natural beauty, they argue, distracts us from our primary love for God. Of course, they have a fair amount of evidence to support their position. Isn't history replete with the stories of those who have fallen away because they were enamored of literature, music, theater, or dance? For too many, aestheticism—a devotion to art as an end in itself—is a kind of substitute religion. Augustine confesses his youthful infatuation with the theater. Even after he became a Christian, he struggled to control his inordinate attraction to food and music. Dante presents the memorable story of a young couple suffering in the Inferno because they fell into carnal sin, "their reason mastered by desire," while reading a racy romance.[1] The number of complaints against the arts (their capacity to corrupt, falsify, lead astray) is large. We should not take these grievances lightly.

Other Christians hold a somewhat ambivalent view of beauty. In this second position are those who maintain that the arts may be suitable for our consumption and enjoyment, as long as they are kept safely out of the church. In this view, the church is a serious domain dedicated to moral and theological matters. The arts, being frivolous or "mere" entertainment, belong to the private or personal sphere. The arts may bring pleasure to one's personal life, but they are more or less irrelevant to the life of the community of faith. I know this position well, for it is the one that I often encountered growing up.

BEAUTY COMES FROM GOD

There are other positions regarding the arts—beyond stark denial and an incoherent dualism. Another position has stood as a major (if not the majority) position for millennia. While conceding that the arts may be abused or misused (as all good gifts can be), this position holds that the arts may fulfill a distinct spiritual purpose in individuals' lives and in the church. According to this view, the arts are to be sponsored, employed, and enjoyed—indeed, celebrated—in the life of the Christian community. In his Arts and Religion Survey, Robert Wuthnow establishes that the arts are closely linked to the spiritual formation of adults.[2] In fact, those who had ample exposure to the arts in childhood are more likely to report spiritual awareness in adulthood. This should not be surprising. After all, God, the Maker of heaven and earth, planted in human beings the gift of creativity and the capacity to desire beauty.

Early theologians commonly noted that God is the artist, craftsman, or architect of creation. "He is the Musician who controls that universal-sounding harmony which He exercises through all the physical world," says Paulinus of Nola.[3] God himself is Beauty (Psalm 27:4), the Source of all beauty, the One who gives men and women the rare gift to experience beauty. Human beings are, according to Paul, God's handiwork or compositions, literally his "poems" (Ephesians 2:10).[4] In other words, we are living works of art creating things in imitation of our Maker. It would be strange, indeed, for the Creator to endow humans with the innate capacity to fashion and appreciate beauty, and then to pronounce this capacity suspect or forbidden.

JESUS, THE GREAT ARTIST

Jesus is the model for how one is to respond to beauty. According to the New Testament, Jesus, the Word or Logos, is the source of creation. If the Father is the Master Builder, then the Son is the supervising architect and agent of Creation:

> for in him all things in heaven and on earth were created, things visible and invisible...;all things have been created through him and for him. He himself is before all things, and in him all things hold to together. (Colossians 1:15-17)

Given this original cosmic assignment, is it not appropriate that Jesus of Nazareth was a craftsman by trade? Having built the universe, it seems fitting that, as a human being, he would turn to building houses or furniture.[5] Jesus, we know, loved beauty and observed nature closely. He could look at a fig tree, a lily, a sparrow, a cloud, a loaf of bread, or a mustard seed—and find a spiritual truth therein. Like all artists, he knew the power of a strong image, a vivid scene, a crisp turn of phrase, or a moving story to rivet, disturb, and astonish. As his parables show, Jesus was a divine poet, the story-telling God.[6]

Where did Jesus get these ideas? Growing up in a Jewish home, he learned the story of Creation from Genesis 1. God's repeated declaration that every created thing is good—and on the last day of creation, "very good"—must have been in his thoughts often. The Psalms, which declare the beauty of Creation, would have been on his lips as well, as he memorized the law and the prophets and as he worshiped in the synagogue:

> O Lord, our Sovereign, how majestic is your name in all the earth! You have set your glory above the heavens....When I look at your heavens, the work

of your fingers, the moon and the stars that you have established; what are
human beings that you are mindful of them...? (Psalm 8:1, 3-5)

He would have often recited Psalm 104:2-5:

You stretch out the heavens like a tent, you set the beams of your chambers
on the waters, you make the clouds your chariot, you ride on the wings of the
wind, you make the winds your messengers, fire and flame your ministers.

Jesus' world, in other words, is like that of the poet Gerard Manley Hopkins:

The world is charged with the grandeur of God.

It will flame out, like shining from shook foil

. . .

Because the Holy Ghost over the bent

World broods with warm breast and with ah! bright wings.

Although the world is "bent" (marred by sin and fallen), it still bears the indelible traces
of the Father's imprint and presence: "a tremor of bliss, a wink of heaven, a whisper," as
T. S. Eliot says it.[7] Such a view naturally leads to an appreciation of beauty. Beauty is not
some superficial thing, not some bauble or an ornament that one can take or leave. As
Bernard Häring explains, beauty is a vital constituent of creation:

To dismiss the beautiful as something superfluous is to make life
miserable, mean, barren. For a Christian who knows and adores God's
glory and majesty, disparagement of the beautiful is betrayal of the Spirit,
for beauty is a splendour of the true and the good....One who, in all his
being, knows truth and knows goodness is already caught by the love of
the beautiful.[8]

Let us state the obvious: God made beauty a fundamental feature of creation. Not to
notice this splendid gift from God is, at best, bad form; at worst, bad faith.

The pilgrim heart, therefore, is deeply, unashamedly attracted to "visible,
audible, embodied beauty."[9] The pilgrim heart rejects outright the Manichean
notion that the physical world is evil, with only the non-material being "spiritual."
The mature disciple distinguishes between "living in the flesh" and living
"according to the flesh".[10] Living in the flesh is a good thing, for it is where God has
squarely placed us. Living according to the flesh is a bad thing because it means one

has preferred a lesser thing (that which God has made) to an infinitely good thing (God himself). The mistake is not in the admiration of beauty, but in the confusion of values. "All things are beautiful because you made them," wrote Augustine; "but you who made everything are inexpressibly more beautiful."[11] With our values in proper order, we can freely enjoy beauty, create beautiful things, and even make beauty a part of our spiritual development.

THE ARTS AND SPIRITUAL GROWTH: TRUTH AND MYSTERY

But how do beauty and the arts help one grow spiritually? The answer is broad, and so I can offer only a few observations. First, the best and greatest art is not only appealing to the eye and ear; it also transmits great and lasting insights. Paul understood this point when he found it appropriate to quote the pagan poets Menander and Epimenides in Acts 17. As the old hymn reminds us, "He shines in all that's fair." Another way of expressing it is: "All truth is God's truth," wherever it may be found.[12] Who hasn't been powerfully moved by a theme or idea in a great story or in a well-acted play or movie? Whether it's a Shakespearean tragedy, a classic novel, or a contemporary comedy, in these one can find wisdom and insight. Sometimes one finds even more: a hint that something spiritual or transcendent may lie beyond the visible world. Joseph Sittler observes: "God is interested in a lot of things besides religion. God is the Lord and Creator of all life, and there are manifestations of the holy in its celebration or in its repudiation—in every aspect of the common life."[13]

A great deal of art actually serves a pre-evangelistic function, preparing the soil in the hearts of men and women, by reminding them of the truth of how bleak and lonely life without God can be. Whenever the arts remind us of our frailty, brokenness, or illness, they implicitly make the case for redemption. A great deal of modern art, for example, confirms human sinfulness and the constant longing for something more and something better. Honest art can serve a diagnostic function by exposing our desperate condition so that we might look for a remedy. Films as varied as *Contact, Babette's Feast, Millions,* and *Chronicles of Narnia* present characters hungry for transcendence and a relationship with something above and beyond this world.[14]

Art can do something else: it can awaken spiritual longing. As Thomas Aquinas noted long ago, beauty is always connected to longing or desire. By definition, "desire is a kind of movement towards something."[15] When I was a child, movies, novels, and music ignited my imagination and fed my desire to know more, see more, and do more than I found within the limits of my small-town life. The arts have this power, says Emily Dickinson:

> There is no frigate like a book
>
> To take us lands away,
>
> Nor any coursers like a page
>
> Of prancing poetry.

As a youth, C. S. Lewis found that music, fairy tales, and Norse legends stirred his longing for something above and beyond. He had a name for this inconsolable longing for the unknown. He called it "joy." The arts activated a desire in Lewis for something ancient and long forgotten, something on the horizon not yet seen. "All joy reminds," Lewis said. "It is never a possession, always a desire for something longer ago or further away or still 'about to be.'"[16] In time this stirring in Lewis found its answer in Jesus Christ. We simply cannot ignore the fact that art was an element in the Oxford don's eventual conversion. It is no surprise, then, that literary art, in Lewis's hands, became the tool of his amazing ministry to the world. More than forty years after his death the best of his books remain bestsellers. Considering the millions of copies of his books read around the world, Lewis may prove to be the most effective evangelist in several hundred years.

Beauty not only stirs a longing for something beyond, it can actually suggest God's presence in our world. Simone Weil felt the sacramental power of art:

> The beauty of the world is Christ's tender smile for us coming through matter....Every true artist has had real, direct, and immediate contact with the beauty of the world, contact that is of the nature of a sacrament. God has inspired every first-rate work of art, though its subject may be entirely secular....[17]

Madeleine L'Engle concurs, suggesting that some art can transport us to "the realm of the numinous." She reminds us that the exquisite chorale "O Sacred Head Now Wounded," from *St. Matthew's Passion*, was once the melody of a popular street song of Bach's day. Yet in the master's hands that pop tune became "one of the most superb pieces of religious music ever written." L'Engle concludes: "There is nothing so secular that it cannot be sacred, and that is one of the deepest messages of the Incarnation."[18]

FAITH AND THE IMAGINATION

Encountering truth, awakening a longing for transcendence, experiencing mystery—for some people, the arts can do all these things. Yet there is another powerful dimension to the arts which must be considered. The arts can cultivate faith through the exercise of the imagination. Some Christians have become suspicious of the imagination due to a misunderstanding of the phrase "vain imaginations" found in Romans 1:21 (King James Version). Some semantic confusion lurks here. Paul's warning against "vain imaginations" is really about the abuse of the mind—that is, futile or dangerous thinking. The Apostle is alerting us to a kind of faulty thinking that willfully ignores the reality of God in the world. We don't abandon thinking merely because some people misuse logic, and we don't renounce imagination because some people misuse their creative powers.

Imagination, properly understood, is a great blessing and even an essential element of faith. Imagination, at its most basic level, is the capacity to envision something unavailable to sight. Faith is similar since it involves the capacity to exercise the mind and the heart to conceive what cannot be experienced through the senses. *Faith, in other words, requires imagination.* Paul even argues for a faithful imagination: "we look not at what can be seen but at what cannot be seen" (2 Corinthians 4:18). A child deprived of imagination may in time find it difficult to trust in an unseen God or hope for a glorious, invisible heaven. This is why ancient Judaism immersed its children in the lore of Jewish history. Israel's stories, rituals, and festivals constantly cultivated a young Jew's imagination to see and experience the story of Exodus with the mind's eye and to envision a future Messianic age. Christian worship and practice offer something equivalent. The great stories of the Bible and the rites of worship, by cultivating the spiritual imagination, make belief possible.

The problem, then, is not imagination as such—but an uncultivated or a badly cultivated imagination. The function of the spiritual disciplines, the very purpose of life in the community of faith, its music, its art, its worship, then, is to bequeath to the members of the community (and to children in particular) an imagination shaped by Scriptural narrative and the great stories of God's heroes. To cede the imagination to the devil is to throw away one of God's most powerful, faith-building gifts. Our calling is to exercise the imagination, not abandon it.

WELCOMING THE ARTISTS AMONG US

The church has not always been kind to its artists. Maturing in communities that ignore or even reject their gifts, some artists, musicians, writers, and actors become discouraged and drift away. Sad to say, sometimes they find a kinder welcome in the world than they do in the church, and the church is the poorer for it. Yet in many ways artists model what it means to have a pilgrim heart. They explore the truth through the medium in which they work. They revere the mystery of creation; they work humbly with their materials, embodying the "restless ache for something beyond," as Lewis called it. Along with the poet Czeslaw Milosz, they say: "In this world there is too much ugliness and horror. So there must be, somewhere, goodness and truth. And that means somewhere God must be."[19] These artists not only inform our minds, they nurture our hearts, for art is more than cognition. It is divine truth recollected in color, shape, and sound. Their art, potentially, at least, becomes a path to a better world.

Skirmishes between believers and the arts have become routine in our day. Ingmar Bergman, himself the son of a Protestant clergyman, rebelled against the church's tendency to dismiss the arts. In his 1982 movie *Fanny and Alexander*, Bergman tells the melancholy story of two bright and eager children who, after their father dies, must leave behind a sumptuous theatrical world of color, light, and laughter in order to reside in a bishop's home that is sterile, dull, and dreary. The movie is a kind of parable, revealing the director's belief that the church stands coolly indifferent to the arts.

Yet it has not always been so. Emil Brunner's reminder is important: "From time immemorial the relation between art and religion has been friendly rather than hostile...." The church and the arts are so deeply connected that "[w]e simply cannot imagine Western Art apart from Christianity."[20] "The sense of beauty...remains rooted in the heart of man as a powerful incentive," observed Weil.[21] Indeed, pilgrim hearts have always understood that creation and creativity are earthly signs ever gesturing towards the Creator. Thankfully, the necessary relationship between artists and the church is undergoing a revival in our day.[22] Artists are being invited to portray the faith of the believers, to paint the scenes, compose the songs, write the plays, and tell the stories that will shape the imaginations and the lives of the next generation.

All who love Scripture should note the obvious: The Bible itself is a majestic work of art. Otherwise, why are the book of Job, the Psalms, and the parables of Jesus rendered in such artful form? God seems forever committed to beauty. Otherwise, the glories of heaven make no sense at all. "Our mission in the world and our final hope are presented in terms of beauty and glory," writes Bernard Häring.[23] Indeed, as John's Revelation makes clear, our eternal dwelling place is characterized by extraordinary beauty: fabulous architecture, poetry, music, song, and liturgy. Despisers of the arts will find heaven a rather odd place to spend eternity. The God who created the world in all its splendor, who placed the sensuous Song of Solomon within the canon of Scripture, and who promises a glorious new heaven and a dazzling new earth, must love beauty. Could it be that life on this earth is but a reflection of, and a preparation for, the superior, lasting beauty of the world to come?

14

FEASTING: MEMORY AND MEALTIMES

This power of memory is great, very great, my God.
It is a vast and infinite profundity.
—Augustine

Do this in remembrance of me.
Luke 22:19

Day by day...they broke bread at home and ate their food
with glad and generous hearts, praising God and
having the goodwill of all the people.
Acts 2:46

What happens when we forget? When people lose their memory through Alzheimer's or other forms of dementia, the familiar becomes foreign. The confidence of identity—who they are and where they are from—erodes. Loved ones recede as strangers take their place, and those closest to the victim experience a creeping alienation as they see a lifetime of memories evaporate.

Likewise, entire groups of people can experience cultural amnesia. When a society forgets, it too experiences disorientation, incoherence, and despair. Augustine's lament might be our own: "I am scattered in times whose order I do not understand. The storms of incoherent events tear to pieces my thoughts, the inmost entrails of my soul...."[1] Through personal recollection and reflection, Augustine understood his role as a player in God's grand story of gracious interaction with human history. His place in the lineage of God's people gave him stability and hope.

Augustine knew what pilgrim hearts have always known—the faithful believer must be steeped in memory, tradition, and history. Knowing their "astonishing point of origin"[2] going back to the beginning of time, they are able to understand where they now stand. Knowing the traditions, pilgrim hearts see through the confusion of the present storms of life. Yet this commitment to memory is not a nostalgic love of a dead past. Among the followers of Jesus there is no interest in building museums to a vanished culture.

At the same time, the believer understands that the past lives on in the present. Just as surely as the DNA of our ancestors plays a role in our present existence, the things that happened in the past continue to play out in our lives, whether we notice or not. Jesus and the writer of the book of Hebrews teach us that the saints of the ages are living, not dead. Daily we walk in an arena surrounded by a vast cloud of living witnesses (Matthew 22:31-32; Hebrews 11:1-12:1). Events of the past are not merely material for textbooks but resources for reflection and current decision-making. We can converse with the past, finding hope in it for the future. What has lovingly been handed to us, we carefully place in the hands of others. Paul calls this "maintain[ing] the traditions" (1 Corinthians 11:2).

The Bible invites us to remember because memory is the great vehicle of spiritual identity and formation, an important supply for moral reflection, and a source for constructing the future. Without memory there can be no mature and enduring spirituality. Memory makes gratitude possible, for thankfulness presupposes the recollection of gifts received. Memory creates identity, for we can hardly know who we are or why we are here if we have no recall of where we have been. As Augustine discovered through rehearsing his own memories, "I meet myself and recall what I am, what I have done, and when and where and how I was affected when I did it."[3] Memory lays the foundation for penitence, for how can we be sorry if our consciences do not remind us of our past transgressions? Lastly, memory makes hope possible. While amnesiacs are trapped in their bewilderment, people with strong memories see possibility. They know that their present condition is not the only option. Memory of God's gracious faithfulness is, indeed, a great treasure house providing confidence and courage when trial or disappointment come their way. People with good memories can say: "Things can be different. Time and history are not fixed."[4]

It is important to understand that memory is not exclusively a private or individual matter. Robert Wilken points out that "[m]emory locates us in the corporate and the particular. There is no memory that is not rooted in communal experience...."[5] As ancient Israel and the early church understood, memory is formed and sustained in a faithful community. According to Walter Brueggemann, the "biblical text has an enormous stake in memory, and the church is the community that gathers to remember."[6]

One of the most notable consequences of modernity has been the erasure of cultural memory. The ideologies of our age have routinely rejected the value of the past. Paradoxically, even some historians approach the past in a way so as to render it irrelevant to our lives.[7] In the last century totalitarian states actively sought to destroy cultural memory. Paul Connerton calls this "organized oblivion" or a forced forgetting.[8] Nazi Germany and the Stalinist states of Eastern Europe carefully rewrote history to suit their political purposes, and writers like Alexander Solzhenitsyn, Elie Wiesel, and Milan Kundera have written to undo the calculated attempts to airbrush from history the stories of whole peoples. Kundera describes this process of forced forgetting:

> The first step in liquidating a people is...to erase its memory. Destroy its books, its culture, its history. Then have somebody write new books, manufacture a new culture, invent a new history. Before long the nation will begin to forget what it is and what it was. The world around will forget even faster.[9]

We might extend this chilling observation to say that the first step in liquidating a religious community is to erase its memory, destroy its books, its culture, its history. And the first step in destroying personal faith is to abandon one's own spiritual heritage.

A remarkable fact about the United States and Western societies in general has been the rapid loss of memory by choice, rather than through government decree. Spiritual and historical amnesia occurs easily, without protest, as scriptural knowledge, church history, and the stories of our own families languish through neglect. North Americans and Europeans are amnesiacs by choice.[10] The insidious thing about amnesia—whether self-imposed or externally enforced—is that once it takes hold, the victims cannot recall what—or even that—they have forgotten. Many Christians today are like Leonard Shelby, the protagonist of the movie *Memento*, who puzzles over notes he's written to himself, some tattooed on his own skin. He can never remember enough, or retain these memories, to know who he is and what has happened to him. Similarly bereft of memory, Christians experience life as a confusing jumble of random sensations and fragmented encounters. They have forgotten that they have forgotten.

There are effective antidotes to spiritual amnesia—Scripture, tradition, and the practices of the community being among them. Scripture teaches that believers should be experts at memory and memory transmission. Indeed, one could say that the Bible is a book of memories as well as a source of instruction on how to transmit memory from one generation to the next. It's never enough for a single member of the community to remember. The whole community must be devoted to passing the story of faith on to the next generation. They do this, in part, by teaching the members of the community to view themselves as actors in a timeless drama. Thus, they view "their predecessors as contemporaries, not objects."[11]

For example, the story of the Exodus from Egypt as passed on by the Hebrews was not merely the story of one's remote ancestors. Jewish boys and girls were taught to cast themselves in this drama of liberation. They recited the speeches in the first person, as their personal story:

> *We* were Pharaoh's slaves in Egypt, but the Lord brought *us* out with a mighty hand. The Lord displayed before *our* eyes great and awesome signs and wonders against Egypt....He brought *us* out from there in order to bring *us* in, to give *us* the land that he promised on oath to *our* ancestors. (Deuteronomy 6:21-23, my emphasis)

Through such collective recitations, believers performed the stories of the community and made them their own. What might have been a stale textbook account became a current event and a personal story, embedded in the hearts of each member of the community.

Something equivalent happens in Christian worship when we read aloud the story of Christ's death and resurrection, or when we sing a familiar hymn like this one by Isaac Watts:

> When I survey the wondrous cross
> On which the prince of glory died,
> My richest gain I count but loss
> And pour contempt on all my pride.
>
> . . .
>
> See, from his Head, His hands, His feet,
> Sorrow and love flow mingled down;
> Did e'er such love and sorrow meet,
> Or thorns compose so rich a crown?

Another example comes whenever we sing, "O sacred head *now* wounded." In these moments of communal recitation we see present before us the bleeding head, the crucified hands, and feet of the One who came to save. Such communal worship practices cultivate what Brueggemann calls a "counterimagination," a way of envisioning reality enabling us to withstand the sterile images offered daily by the surrounding secular culture.

REMEMBERING THROUGH FEASTS

People living in less developed cultures often lack the tools of modernity such as books, libraries, literacy, and advanced technology; yet, paradoxically, they may preserve and transmit cultural memory better than "advanced" cultures. In *How Societies Remember* Paul Connerton demonstrates that traditional cultures know why the stories are important to their well-being, and they remember how to transmit them to succeeding generations.

One of the most ancient and effective remembering practices is the shared meal. It is striking how prominent meals are in Scripture—Moses with the seventy elders on the mountainside, Jesus eating with his followers, the disciples on the road to Emmaus, the love feasts of the early church. Eating is referred to in Scripture as much as or more than believing is. Jesus often uses the meal as a fitting symbol of spiritual harmony and union with God: "Blessed is anyone who will eat bread in the kingdom of God!" (Luke 14:15). Table fellowship is taken to be a deeply spiritual matter: "Listen! I am standing at the door, knocking; if you hear my voice and open the door, I will come in to you and eat with you, and you with me" (Revelation 3:20). At table, covenants are ratified, relationships restored, and memories embedded (literally in the physical body and in the "body" of the community). The communal meals and feasts in Scripture (Passover, Eucharist, love feasts, etc.) are essential commemorative habits.

The earliest Christians devoted enormous attention to meals including the Eucharist or the Lord's Supper and communal meals called agapé or love feasts. The latter brought together not only food, but prayers, Scripture reading, and hymn singing. The fact is that in early Christianity there was a deep and mysterious fusion of food and faith that we only dimly understand in an age which so relentlessly segregates the sacred and the secular. I remember as a young Bible reader trying to distinguish between the meals mentioned so often in the New Testament. Which ones were "secular" meals and which ones were "sacred"? I had to give up my flawed project because in the Bible food talk is really God talk.[12]

At the feast the body and all its senses are involved—listening to conversation and story, the aromas and flavors of food and drink, the sights of smiles and gestures, the holding of hands in blessing, the sounds of music and song. No wonder feasts were arranged when biblical characters wanted to memorialize an important occasion, such as when the father welcomed home the prodigal son. We must recognize the obvious: communal meals have the same power today to stir hearts and confirm our memories as they did in ancient times. As Jeff Smith explains:

> Feasting is closely related to memory. We eat certain things in a particular way in order to remember who we are....Consider your own childhood. Think of the very best times that you shared with your family and I am sure that the dining-room table will come to mind. Remember the smell of the

kitchen. Close your eyes and smell those aromas, those memories. The brain remembers odors and smells and scents better than just about anything else. Lin Yutang, the great philosopher, put it this way, "What is patriotism except the memories of the good things that we ate as a child?"

....If a culture ceases to feast, and ours nearly has, will it cease to be a culture? I think so....It is very obvious that TV dinners have no memories![13]

Because communal meals are laden with emotion and memory, any community (whether church or family) wishing to be serious about the transmission of its values will give special attention to meals. They will not let the frenetic pace of life, the commitment to after-school activities and long hours at work get in the way of shared meals. The alternative, the neglect of mealtimes, so common today, risks robbing the next generation of the "endless overflow of communication" that generates familial and spiritual memory.[14]

When I consider what shaped me spiritually, I must give considerable credit to the effect of communal meals. I remember church gatherings that were preceded by or followed by large dinners in which everyone participated. I remember large family gatherings on Sundays and weekdays in which the whole family and sometimes members of our extended family joined us at the table. These meals were not elaborate, but they were powerful in their capacity to generate common memories that will last me a lifetime. We were not affluent, but we were rich in community.

STRAWBERRIES, BREAD, AND JESUS

While in college, our older son, Kyle, made a prospective mission trip to Romania. When he arrived at the Bucharest train station, he was unable to locate the missionary who was to meet him. Hours passed, and Kyle did not know what to do. He had no way to reach the missionary. As the afternoon turned to evening, he stood under a streetlight, reading a book, hoping the man would arrive. As night fell, an old woman approached our son. Though she could speak no English, and Kyle knew no Romanian, she gestured to him to come to her house. Lonely, hungry, and a little desperate, he didn't know what else to do, so he went home with her. In her rather spartan apartment, she prepared him a simple meal that included a few strawberries with a dusting of sugar. Clearly she was offering her best. Later, the woman's English-speaking daughter came home and learned our son's problem. Eventually Kyle found his way. I have often thought about that nameless woman who extended such unexpected courtesy to this foreigner, my son, who did not speak her language; and I have been chastened to consider whether I would have done the same had I been in her situation. The one I proclaim to be my Lord said, "I was hungry and you gave me food, I was thirsty and you gave me something to drink, I was a stranger and you welcomed me..." (Matthew 25:35).

It is remarkable how simple, material objects can occasion the holiest of moments. A cup of cold water, a slice of bread, strawberries with just a little sugar—through such small things the God of the universe sometimes reveals himself to us. As the disciples in Emmaus discovered, Jesus could make himself known in the breaking of the bread. While it is true that we do not live by bread alone, the very breaking of bread often becomes holy: "If the gift is rightly given and rightly received, the passing of a morsel of bread from one person to another is something like real communion."[15]

15

READING AND STORYTELLING: HOW NARRATIVE BUILDS FAITH

Tell me the story of Jesus,
Write on my heart ev'ry word.
—Fanny J. Crosby

Did God...not invent man so that He might hear him tell tales?
—George Steiner

There are, of course, many vehicles of memory. Most prominent in my mind are Bible reading, storytelling, and reading—the common denominator of these three being the way they preserve memory through narrative. An abundant and growing body of evidence shows that stories have a unique capacity to transmit values, shape identity, move people to action, and preserve memory. For this reason, people who care about the next generation will be experts at telling the community's story. They will preserve and celebrate the stories that develop character, transmit the community's beliefs, and inspire the young to understand their connection to the community. They will give the next generation good stories to live by, and they will fiercely protect their young against toxic narratives that poison and weaken us.[1]

If scriptural memory is to survive, we must reassert the centrality of the Bible's stories to the life of the Christian community, and we must consider whether our current ways of reading Scripture feed memory or not. In the Jewish tradition, the goal of Bible reading is "to make the past actual, to form a solidarity with the fathers."[2] The same goal—to make the biblical past alive in our hearts—should govern the Christian's approach to Scripture. Of course, it is appropriate that we also read Scripture for instruction (2 Timothy 3:16-17); however, lists of rules hardly evoke passion or powerful memory. We remember poorly those things that do not have personal meaning (random lists of numbers or long lists of do's and don't's, for example). We tend to remember well-told stories or events which we have personally experienced. No doubt this is why much of the Bible is rendered in story form, and no doubt this is why we should read the Bible somewhat like a play script, in which we have a speaking part.

If the goal of Scripture is changed lives and transformed hearts, then we should give considerable thought to *how* we read, understand, and apply the Word. Paul implies one way when he invites Timothy to consider scriptural meaning in the light of the autobiographical narratives of the dear people who taught him the faith—Paul himself, as well as his mother and grandmother (2 Timothy 1:5; 3:10-17). Scripture, biography, and autobiography should be connected, Paul implies.

As we move deeper into Scripture, we should freely use the many tools for Bible learning that are at our fingertips. Every bookstore offers annotated Bibles, commentaries, Bible dictionaries, and a wealth of other tools for understanding the Bible, for which we should be grateful. The historical, critical, and grammatical tools for discovering textual meaning are truly wonderful. Probably at no time since the Bible was written have we had a better chance of gaining accurate understandings of the Bible's meaning. While these study tools are helpful, they are not enough. Without neglecting them, I wish to suggest that there are additional practices—perhaps we should call them "postures" of reading—that open up textual meaning.

For example, we would do well to read with a spirit of humility and openness. We can also read with personal investment and passion. (We can say with the Psalmist, "This I know, that God is for me." Psalm 56:9) Scripture contains a story deeply relevant to the plot of our own lives.[3] I am suggesting a prayerful or meditative approach that connects the biblical narrative with our own.[4] For an illustration, consider how one might approach a text like the 23rd Psalm. We might ask whether this psalm is:

- A word from God spoken to us (a revelation)
- A word spoken by us to others (an exhortation)
- A word about God (instruction)
- A word spoken by us to God (a communal prayer)

Of course, Psalm 23 is all of these things—revelation, exhortation, instruction, and prayer. It is certain that its instruction or revelation will be more complete—and life changing—if we read it contemplatively and prayerfully. In a prayerful reading, sometimes called *lectio divina*,[5] one reads not only with one's mind, "but in a certain sense with one's whole being." It involves "the orientation of our whole body, mind and spirit to God in silence, attention, and adoration." Rather than reading Scripture to correct others or win arguments, the focus is on one's own need to change; there is a *"conversion of our entire self to God."*[6]

In the 23rd Psalm we witness the faith and hope of King David. Yet, as we meditate on the text, it ceases to be solely an "objective" historical account of another person's struggle to believe and trust. The reader walks into this psalm and makes it his or her own. God is my shepherd, and I proclaim him so. This attitude allows me to savor the times he has restored my soul after the great tempests in my life, to recall how he has walked with me in the deathly shadows. As the text seeps into my innermost being, God invites me to reprise the events of my own story—when I feared evil and when I did not; when I was comforted and when I felt alone; when I felt humiliation as well as vindication. Through David's words, I am led to the threshold of the future where I declare my commitment to stay true to him forever.

This psalm, then, is a word from God, but it is also my word spoken back to God. It becomes a mysteriously circular prayer in which God's breath in me returns to the Source of all breath. Reading the Word melds into prayer, and the heart goes on pilgrimage, as George Herbert describes it:

> Prayer the Church's banquet, angels' age,
>
> God's breath in man returning to his birth,
>
> The soul in paraphrase, heart in pilgrimage.
>
> The Christian plummet sounding heav'n and earth;
>
> Engine against th' Almighty, sinners' tower,

> Reversèd thunder, Christ-side-piercing spear,
> The six-days' world transposing in an hour,
> A kind of tune, which all things hear and fear;
> Softness, and peace, and joy, and love, and bliss,
> Exalted manna, gladness of the best,
> Heaven in ordinary, man well dressed,
> The milky way, the bird of Paradise,
> Church-bells beyond the stars heard, the soul's blood,
> The land of spices; something understood.[7]

In this way of reading, Scripture becomes prayer and prayer turns into creative communion with God. Something happens beyond words or reason. The reader enters a transcendent place: "the milky way," "beyond the stars." What happens we cannot exactly say. It is "something understood."

This prayerful kind of reading can work with many passages of Scripture. I've long thought that the story of the disciples on the road to Emmaus is ready-made for this method of reading (Luke 24:13-35). Depending on the occasion, the text prompts me to ask: Am I the host in a relationship with an unseen guest (the risen Christ)? Or am I the guest who is welcomed by the Stranger? Do I doubt, as the Emmaus travelers did? Are my eyes open to Messiah, or is he hidden from me by doubt, confusion, or depression? Do the words of Jesus touch and burn within my heart? If so, how should I respond to them? Is this only a curious, ancient tale or a contemporary plot in which I am implicated? Are these words true *for me*?

If I sit humbly in silence with this episode from Luke's Gospel, if I listen and pray these words, letting them slowly sink into my heart, then I am engaging in a form of Scripture reading which Christians have practiced for centuries. Jesus promised that if we love him and keep his word, then he and the Father will come make their home with us or in us (John 14:23).

When they hear about a "spiritual" reading of Scripture, some students of the Bible, especially those trained in a rationalistic tradition, become worried. They suppose that a "subjective" approach to Scripture will lead to fanciful or highly eccentric interpretations. While the fear is understandable, there are protections against strange, radically unorthodox readings. First, the prayerful reading of Scripture can be balanced by other, more traditional ways of approaching the text. One can read "spiritually" as well as analytically. Furthermore, reading with others in community provides a strong check against idiosyncratic readings. Within Judaism there is a long-honored tradition of reading Torah with one's *hevruta*, that is, one's study partner (from the Hebrew root *haver/havera* "friend"). Whether with a single study partner or within a friendship circle, one reads the text slowly, carefully, meditatively—checking one's insights against the wisdom of the community. The goal is to encounter the Word together, much like Philip and the Ethiopian treasurer practiced it (Acts 8:26-40). Because Scripture is the Word of God for the whole church, the church provides discernment and correction to unwarranted readings. This has always been the normative way Christians have read Scripture.

SUSTAINING THE HEART THROUGH STORY

There are other ways believers remember their spiritual heritage—for example, through stories found in ordinary books that fill our libraries. Human beings seem hard-wired for story. A good story affects our values, identity, and minds in ways that a list of bare facts never can. One could say that it is the storytellers in any culture who have the greatest influence on the direction of a culture, not its legislators, government leaders, or scholars.

Some stories, I firmly believe, should be transmitted orally or in writing, not visually. As anyone knows who has listened to a good storyteller like Garrison Keillor, oral tales can move us and lodge deeply in our memories. We are fortunate if we had a parent, an uncle, or a grandmother who made a lasting impression on us through a cracking good tale. Stories, whether read or told, exercise the mind's picture-making capacity better than the most creative movie set designers or studio animators. Motion pictures, good as they are, have one serious limitation: by doing most of the picturing for us, they can limit our freedom to imagine for ourselves. This is why readers are often disappointed when they watch a movie version of a favorite book. Wolfgang Iser lays down an important principle: "we can only picture things which are not there."[8] As I write these words I am looking out a window on the Santa Monica Mountains. Because I can see these mountains as I write, I cannot visualize them. If imagination requires the visualization of things not present, then the parent who hopes to encourage her children's imagination may be wise to strategically limit their access to movies and TV.

The relevance of this discussion to faith formation should be clear, since faith "convinces us of realities that we do not see" (Hebrews 11:1, Revised English Bible). "[W]e look not at what can be seen but at what cannot be seen" (2 Corinthians 4:18). If we could see "all," we might be omniscient, but we would not be faithful. ("[F]or we walk by faith and not by sight"—2 Corinthians 5:7.) Thus, children deprived of oral tales and ample amounts of reading may actually be inhibited in their capacity to develop faith. George Steiner's warning deserves our consideration:

> To starve a child of the spell of the story, of the canter of the poem, oral or written, is a kind of living burial....A comic book is better than nothing so long as there is in it the multiplying life of language....If the child is left empty of texts, in the fullest sense of that term, he will suffer an early death of the heart and of the imagination.[9]

Recently I heard of a father who asked his son if he would like to go play baseball. The son replied, "Sure. I'll go get the game card." When video games, TV, and movies substitute for human contact, face-to-face dialogue, and experiences in the natural world, the developing heart of faith is wounded.

Before leaving this subject, one important qualification is in order. For millions of people today (children especially), books and movies do not compete with each other but function in a friendly, complementary way. For example, a new generation is discovering the wonder of C. S. Lewis's fiction because they first saw a captivating movie version of one of the *Chronicles of Narnia (The Lion, the Witch, and the Wardrobe)*. Even many adults are reading Lewis's books (for example, *The Screwtape Letters* and *Mere Christianity*) because a movie piqued their curiosity. There are believers in Hollywood today who are producing movies hoping, in part, to inspire audiences to return to spiritual and character-building literature. We can be thankful when movies introduce people to good books.

READING FOR FAITH

Reading has the power to develop us morally and spiritually by giving us life-altering memories.[10] This is preeminently true of the Bible, of course. But it can also be true of other books outside the canon of Scripture. Augustine, as a young man, read a book on virtue written by Cicero and was so moved by it that it led to his eventual conversion.[11] Simone Weil recited over and over again a beautiful devotional poem—George Herbert's "Love (III)." This poem awakened in the young woman a profound sense of God's gracious hospitality, prompting her conversion.[12] Though these examples are exceptional, through the years I have seen how books influence lives, including my own. For decades I have taught works that bear out this capacity for words and stories to change people. While reading Augustine, Pascal, Tolstoy, George MacDonald, Frederick Buechner, C. S. Lewis, Dietrich Bonhoeffer, and others, some of my students have reported being deeply affected. I recall one student who was in an improper relationship with her boyfriend when she started reading Augustine's *Confessions*. At first, Laurie[13] was upset with Augustine's "puritanical" views on sex. She registered her anger towards Augustine in her journal, which she allowed me to read. In time, though, Augustine's struggle with sexual desire ("Lord, make me chaste—but not yet") affected Laurie's understanding of herself and her responsibility. Before the semester was over, she ended the relationship and made a new start.

Not all readers respond so dramatically to texts, of course, but the point is that some do find themselves mysteriously moved by great works. The power of literature is confirmed by the tendency of dictators to try to control the press. They know that words generate ideas, ideas lead to action, and action can unleash revolutions. John Milton, himself a revolutionary, celebrated the power of books: "For books are not absolutely dead things, but do contain a potency of life in them to be as active as that soul whose progeny they are....[A] good book is the precious life-blood of a master spirit, embalmed and treasured up on purpose to a life beyond life."[14] As with any powerful force, books represent risk and danger. Though books can challenge and disturb us in constructive ways, they can also misdirect and undermine; hence, the importance of wide reading and the assimilation of books within a community, with spiritual guides at our side. While many things can shape us—pictures, music, and the other arts—"it does seem to be words that rap most surely at the door."[15]

REMEMBERING THE FUTURE

One special matter deserves attention before we close the discussion. While there are many practices that encourage memory, not all the resulting memories will be pleasant. I think of those who have experienced injuries in their early years that have healed slowly, or perhaps not at all. I picture the son or daughter who endured an abusive home or the young mother who was traumatized by a bad marriage; they hardly feel keen about remembering the past. When the past haunts or hurts us, what do we do?

Interestingly, Scripture presents a startling "yes" and "no" regarding memory. It teaches us both to remember and to forget: "Remember the former things of old," the Lord says in Isaiah 46:9. Yet in the same book, a few chapters later, God instructs us to forget: "For I am about to create new heavens and a new earth; *the former things shall not be remembered or come to mind*" (Isaiah 65:17-18, my emphasis). How can we do both: remember and forget?

The first step is to distinguish between what we should forget (or let go) and what we must remember (or hold on to). However, if we are too close to matters, we may not know the difference. We need perspective, which comes by taking the long view of events. Yet our tendency is to do the opposite—to focus narrowly on our old wounds or our present disappointments. Without the long view, we simply cannot see what is happening to us. It is as though we walked into a movie at mid-point, watched three minutes of it, then walked out. Without any sense of the beginning or the ending, we misread the segment we did see. Scripture invites us to view the whole plot, not merely the small scene that happens to be our own. If we experienced a tragic episode in our lives, God does not demand a literal forgetting, but he does invite a reinterpretation or a reframing of our experience in light of the larger plot which God, the great Director, is unfolding.[16] By reframing our past and "remembering" the future, we see our story in a proper light. Frederick Buechner writes:

> We cannot undo our old mistakes or their consequences any more than we can erase old wounds that we have both suffered and inflicted, but through the power that memory gives us of thinking, feeling, imagining our way back through time we can at long last finally finish with the past in the sense of removing its power to hurt us and other people and stunt our growth as human beings.[17]

Long before any Hollywood director conceived such a complex plot, the Lord sketched a surprising human story, in which the earliest events would anticipate later happenings, and the later happenings would recall earlier events. The Master Storyteller says: "for I am God, and there is no other; I am God, and there is no one like me, declaring the end from the beginning and from ancient times things not yet done" (Isaiah 46:9-10). Even in the very first scene of the "movie" called human history God planted a brief allusion to a later episode (see Genesis 3:15). And for us Johnny-come-latelies in the twenty-first century, he connects our late arrival with events that happened even before Genesis opens, even before the foundations of the earth; and our story is tethered to a glorious future consummation (see Ephesians 1:4; Revelation 21:1-4). However brief our scene on the world's stage, it is meaningfully situated in the full, sacred narrative.

God grants the gift of scriptural memory to the pilgrim heart. Through memory we know a remote past, even if we have not seen it with our eyes, and we contemplate a glorious future yet to be revealed. Such leaps of spiritual imagination liberate us from any egocentric (or tragic) notion that our brief moment on life's stage is the whole story. It is not. No matter what our misfortune might be, it is only a "slight momentary affliction" compared to the "eternal weight of glory beyond all measure" that awaits us in the final episode (2 Corinthians 4:17).

The gift of memory helps in many ways. It gives us our deep sense of chosenness. It confirms our mission to be a blessing in the lives of all whom we meet, and it illuminates our purposes in the dark times. The means of memory are diverse— communal meals, Scripture, storytelling, and good books are among the most powerful. While the forces of cultural amnesia are pervasive in our day, we have many potent habits of memory at our disposal. Indeed, all of the spiritual practices described in this book can create, shape, and give life to our memories. When we make use of these practices, we remember our true story, stay on course, and find our way home.

16

SUFFERING: THE FIRE
THAT PURIFIES

I bring my grief to Thee, the grief I cannot tell.
—Francis Havergal

You have kept count of my tossings; put my tears in your bottle.
Are they not in your record?
Psalm 56:8

Have mercy on some who are wavering.
Jude 22

I live on a university campus situated on a Southern California mountainside overlooking the Pacific Ocean. The potential for danger—whether earthquakes, mudslides, brush fires, or even tsunamis—is well known. The university has teams of people who prepare year-round for disasters. We stockpile food, water, fuel, and medical supplies in the event of a major crisis. We routinely go through drills in order to prepare ourselves for events we hope never occur. These exercises, while time-consuming and costly, are good for us. They keep us alert and nimble. Our campus is safer because we regularly practice for difficult times.

Sometimes I think our campus drills stand as an analogy to what believers do spiritually, both before and after difficulty strikes. Just as our campus never chooses disaster, believers never choose suffering. Rather, suffering chooses us. Suffering is not a good to be sought or a "spiritual practice" in the way that welcoming the stranger, singing, praying, confessing, and forgiving are spiritual practices. Yet no discussion of spirituality would be complete without some attention to "disaster preparedness" in our daily lives. This includes "practicing" for difficult times and learning how difficulty can activate a series of spiritual practices that inspire patience, courage, endurance, and deeper faith. While suffering is not a discipline in the ordinary sense of the term, it is often a significant catalyst in the maturation of the pilgrim heart.

THE WOUNDS OF GRACE

Pain is not always all bad. Everyone can recall something that once seemed difficult, unfortunate, or even tragic, in the short run, but proved a blessing in the long run. Athletes live by the adage "no pain, no gain" and their rigorous training, including pushing beyond the pain, produces better performers on the field or court. Likewise, students know that diligent, sometimes wearying attention to their studies gives them a greater chance at success. Virtuoso musicians are wise enough to appreciate that they can only benefit from long hours of practice. Indeed, all great accomplishments require perseverance and at least some measure of ascetic self-denial. The Bible, echoing this fact, teaches Christians that suffering is often the prelude to something glorious. Just as the pain of childbirth gives way to the joy of new life, so the whole creation is going through painful "labor" as it moves towards some future ecstasy of healing and wholeness:

> We know that the whole creation has been groaning in labor pains until now; and not only the creation, but we ourselves, who have the first fruits of the Spirit, groan inwardly while we wait for adoption, the redemption of our bodies. (Romans 8:22-23)

> For this slight momentary affliction is preparing us for an eternal weight of glory beyond all measure….(2 Corinthians 4:17)

Indeed the cross is shorthand declaring that loss is the way to gain, that defeat is the way to victory, that death itself is not to be feared because it too shall die. As the prayer attributed to Francis of Assisi declares, "It is in dying that we are born to eternal life."

Macrina Wiederkehr, through an imaginative first-person narration, retells the experience of the impoverished woman who endured hemorrhages for twelve long years (Luke 8:43-48):

> Once there was a wound
>
> It was no ordinary wound
>
> It was my wound
>
> We lived together long.

The woman's wound prompts her to find the Great Physician who heals her. The poem concludes with the woman not only describing her healed body, but her grateful heart:

> Trembling I was called forth
>
>   to claim my wholeness.
>
> The bleeding had left me.
>
> The believing remained
>
> And strange as this may sound
>
> I have never lost my gratitude
>
>   for the wound
>
>   that made me so open
>
>   to grace.[1]

Without the years of suffering, would this woman have known such grace? Her attitude may seem exceptional, but it is not. Through the centuries, many believers have thanked God for the wounds which became the means of grace. While it may take a lifetime to arrive at this point of maturity, the pilgrim heart comes to trust that God is the healer who transforms our wounds, our losses, and our griefs into something beautiful.

"WHERE IS GOD IN ALL THIS?"[2]

Life would not be so difficult if we could always see the hand of God at work in our troubled lives. Instead, sometimes it is not at all clear how our present troubles are part of some grand, redemptive purpose. What about those who seek healing and don't find it? Gideon speaks for many of us when, with refreshing candor, he asks the angel who has come calling: *"But, sir, if the Lord is with us, why then has all this happened to us?"* (Judges 6:13, my emphasis). We might well add our voices and ask why the thousands who die in wars, epidemics, and earthquakes? Why the Holocaust and the killing fields of Southeast Asia and Africa? Why the deaths of innocent children from AIDS or leukemia? Each reader could add his or her question to the list: Why the seemingly gratuitous pain in the lives of those I love? Do all woundings and disasters open us to grace? And when we cry to God, and he appears to hide his face from us, what then?[3] Where is the pattern? Where is God?

When such questions arise (whether among others or within our own troubled hearts), we must tread softly and speak slowly. Otherwise, we may— like Job's pious and overly confident friends—compound the hurt by offering glib and tidy answers. Before we propose answers, we must listen and consider where we are, what we feel, and who we are addressing. We can practice the ministry of presence by respecting the anguish of those who say, "I'm hurt and in pain, give me space for healing and mountain air" (Psalm 69, *The Message*).

Years ago, I learned something important about pastoral care from a theologian, Marjorie Suchocki, who emphasized the importance of paying close attention to the state of those to whom I would presume to minister. She explained that the answers to the toughest questions, even if they are theologically correct, may actually be hurtful, if delivered at the wrong time. She emphasized that some answers are good only in the "daytime," while other answers are good in the "night." If a person is in profound pain, an argument that "explains" the suffering (a "daytime" answer) may do little good and potentially much harm. Shakespeare's Edgar, deep in despair at the end of *King Lear*, speaks for all great sufferers:

> The weight of this sad time we must obey;
>
> Speak what we feel, not what we ought to say.

People in the "day"—that is, those who are free of pain or doubt—can enjoy the luxury of speaking what they "ought" to say. They can entertain rational arguments which "explain" why there is evil in a world or suffering in someone else's life. But people in the "night" typically need something other than rational explanation. More than answers, they need care; and they need the emotional, spiritual, and physical presence of loved ones. Because suffering is an intensifier which often attacks reason and isolates the individual, "daytime" answers often sound irrelevant or even hurtful. To be told that one's deepest affliction is "not really so bad," or that "it will soon be all right," or that "God is in control,"— even if such claims be true—can provoke puzzlement, resentment, and anger in the sufferer.[4]

Listening silence and faithful presence may offer far more to the sufferer than daytime explanations. This is not to say that Job's friends were entirely bad theologians. Indeed, some of their advice to Job sounds conventionally orthodox. But their pious lectures pierced Job's heart like poisonous daggers. Jude's counsel (Jude 22) will keep us from sounding like these friends:

Be merciful to those who doubt. (New International Version)

There are some doubting souls who need your pity. (Revised English Bible)

When there are some who have doubts, reassure them. (Jerusalem Bible)

Go easy on those who hesitate in the faith. (The Message)

This exhortation may have been written by a former doubter, the brother of Jesus, who did not become a disciple until after Jesus' resurrection (cf. Matthew 13:55). If so, Jude knew in deeply personal terms why patience with the troubled is prudent.

Recently I heard of a young man who had expressed some honest doubts to members of his congregation. The church members were so disturbed by the man's questions that they simply excommunicated him. How much better it would have been if they had shown a little compassion, a little patience. Flannery O'Connor's insight is capable of helping doubters much more than any scolding:

I think there is no suffering greater than what is caused by the doubts of those who want to believe. I know what torment this is, but I can only see it, in myself anyway, as the process by which faith is deepened....What people don't realize is how much religion costs. They think faith is a big electric blanket, when of course it is the cross. It is much harder to believe than not to believe. If you can't believe, you must at least do this: keep an open mind. Keep it open toward faith, keep wanting it, keep asking for it, and leave the rest to God.[5]

Indeed, questioning is often a necessary station on the road to great faith. Merton writes:

> Only the man who has had to face despair is really convinced that he needs mercy. Those who do not want mercy never seek it. It is better to find God on the threshold of despair than to risk our lives in a complacency that has never felt the need of forgiveness. A life that is without problems may literally be more hopeless than one that always verges on despair.[6]

Through the years I have been blessed by faithful friends who have not merely tolerated, but welcomed, my questions. In their hospitable company something quite unexpected happened. The doubts grew less fierce in the warm glow of their welcome. When I saw that my toughest questions did not rattle or unsettle them, I became more settled and less doubtful. Airing the doubts, I have found, does not enlarge them—just the reverse.

As a teacher, I have tried through the years to extend a similar patient courtesy to my students. I have often told my classes that there are no questions that cannot be asked. Wondering and wandering may be necessary to spiritual discovery whereas making doubts taboo only ensures that they grow stronger. With John Donne, Flannery O'Connor and Alfred Lord Tennyson as my witnesses, I have advised my students:

> Doubt wisely; in strange way
> To stand inquiring, is not to stray. (Donne)
> Even in the life of a Christian, faith rises and falls like the tides of an invisible sea. (O'Connor)
> There lives more faith in honest doubt,
> Believe me, than in half the creeds. (Tennyson)[7]

This advice is not as easy to follow as it may seem. When we desperately want others, especially those most dear to us, to believe, it is often hard to grant them the space to question and to work things through. We want to see them arrive at the shining destination by the shortest route. Yet one of the finest gifts we can give strugglers is the freedom to take the long way 'round. Jesus promises us that if we ask, we will receive; if we search, we will find; if we knock, the door will be opened (Matthew

7:7-11). A good question to ask ourselves is this: *Do we trust Jesus on this point?*

Today, we see the phenomenon of the "helicopter" parent, the slang term for the super soccer moms or dads, who plan, control, and hover over every aspect of their children's lives, even through the college years. There's a version of this in the church today—spiritual overseers who seek to root out every problem or suppress every question. Augustine's mother, Monica, was perhaps the first example in history of the helicopter parent/spiritual guide. She not only prayed for her son during his wayward years, she tried to micromanage his life, even attempting to shadow him in his adult years to guarantee his spiritual safety. In one celebrated episode, Augustine gave his mother the slip by secretly boarding a ship at night, sailing from North Africa to Italy without her knowledge.[8]

On another occasion Monica went to the bishop of her church and begged him to intervene because she saw her son slipping into theological error. Despite her pleading, the church leader would not intercede, possibly because he sensed the youth's resistance to instruction. Augustine needed time and space. Unfazed by the bishop's counsel, the desperate mother continued to beg him to take measures. Exasperated, he told her, "Go away from me: as you live, it cannot be that the son of these tears should perish."[9] Monica reluctantly took the wise man's advice, praying for her son, but also giving him space to reflect, search, and grow. In time, Augustine became a great church leader and one of the greatest theologians of all time. Every anxious parent can learn something from Monica and the bishop— patience immersed in prayers and tears may win one to the faith more quickly than an arsenal of arguments.

Space for questioning is not enough. Sometimes, there must even be permission to protest. In the darkness and the confusion, when the answers do not arrive in timely fashion, anger and doubt often erupt. At such times, the choices are few: suppress the questioning in order to preserve the pious illusion that all is well, or cry out in protest. Within Judaism there is a long tradition allowing people of faith to argue directly with God. Abraham Heschel writes:

> The refusal to accept the harshness of God's ways in the name of his love
> was an authentic form of prayer. Indeed, the ancient Prophets of Israel

were not in the habit of consenting to God's harsh judgment and did not simply nod, saying, "Thy will be done." They often challenged him, as if to say, "Thy will be changed." They often countered and even annulled divine decrees....A man who lived by honesty could not be expected to suppress his anxiety when tormented by profound perplexity. He had to speak out audaciously.[10]

Job, of course, is the greatest example of this tradition. The book that bears his name is a sober warning to the "friends of God" who insist on defending the deity's honor against questions and doubts. If we do not grant freedom to sufferers to feel what they feel and doubt what they doubt, we risk joining Job's nervous friends who, utterly puzzled by Job's desolation, can only explain his problem in one way. The sufferer must have committed some terrible sin that brought down God's wrath upon him. As the story turns out, the friends' hypothesis was wrong. Job's catastrophe was not a consequence of his sin. As the great book ends, God displays anger against Job's friends, for, he says to them: "you have not spoken of me what is right, as my servant Job has done" (42:8). People today who confidently declare that disaster X or Y is the handiwork of God, or who presume to know God's precise intentions, may be in greater spiritual danger than the anguished doubter.[11]

As in our own time, people in Jesus' day commonly thought that bad things only happened to bad people, so they asked Jesus: Is suffering proof of the victim's sin? Each time, Jesus said it was not necessarily so. After Pilate cruelly murdered some Galileans—Jesus' own countrymen who had been offering sacrifices in the temple—the disciples wonder whose sin provoked the massacre. Yet Jesus made it clear these deaths were not the consequence of the victims' sins. He further told the disciples that when "acts of God" occurred, as when a tower at the Pool of Siloam fell, killing eighteen people, no one in particular was at fault: "do you think they were worse offenders than all the others living in Jerusalem? No, I tell you...." (Luke 13:1-5). On yet another occasion his followers asked whose sin caused a particular man to be blind from birth. Like simple moral detectives, the disciples had already narrowed the suspect list down to the parents or the victim himself, but Jesus rejected their conclusion, saying neither the blind man nor the parents were responsible (John 9:1-4).

Jesus refuses to give a definitive explanation of evil. Instead, through teaching and action he demonstrates how one should respond to great misfortune. Instead of merely refuting the disciples' bad theories about the origin of evil (which he does), he goes a step further by providing a positive answer through concrete action. Rather than dwell on a metaphysical question, he restores sight to the blind man. It may be intellectually satisfying to know the origin of murderous dictators and devastating storms, but the pilgrim heart understands that bringing aid and comfort is the best response to the problem of evil.

Anne Lamott describes a time when she walked into a minister's office, utterly bereft of hope. "I could no longer imagine how God could love me," she writes. Seeing how hopeless she was and that her own efforts to reach God were not working, the minister gave her strange advice. He told her to stop praying for awhile and to let him pray for her. Soon after, she began to get better.[12] This minister was not opposed to prayer—far from it. But he did understand that Lamott needed someone to stand with her in her pain and allow her to "live the questions," as the poet Rilke calls it. In so doing, he became a witness to hope.

Those in the night cannot see the light, even if there is light. That is why it is crucial that those who bask in faith should stand with the sufferer, witnessing to hope that may be temporarily invisible. Because we are a body composed of many members, we can "cover" for each other in times of spiritual distress. If I injure my hand or eye, I do not blame either for their poor functioning. Similarly, when someone is in a spiritual crisis we do not judge or condemn; we stand with them and carry some of the weight. This capacity to carry one another's burdens is especially evident in shared worship. Kathleen Norris tells the story of the Benedictine sister who is sustained by the worshiping community: "In the really hard times...when it's all I can do to keep breathing, it's still important for me to go to choir. I feel as if the others are keeping my faith for me, pulling me along."[13] There is a Jewish custom, *se'udat havra'ah*, the meal of replenishment, which is practiced during the period of mourning after the death of a loved one. After returning from the cemetery, the mourner is not supposed to serve others or take food for herself. Other people feed her, symbolizing the way the community nourishes and sustains the mourner in her grief.[14] Solidarity with the pain is the beginning of the healing, Henri Nouwen has said.

Because we follow the One who knew the shadows of Gethsemane and the anguish of the cross, we respect and care for those who experience the dark night of the soul. We are not afraid to bind up the wounds of the afflicted or walk with those who have known God's absence. We may even pray that brutally honest prayer with them: "I believe, help my unbelief!" (Mark 9:24). Pilgrim hearts feel no immediate need to justify the ways of God to man or woman. They are at home with the complexity and mystery of life. They are able to listen and wait as well as take decisive and courageous action.

WE ALL COME TO OUR KNEES

In the face of affliction, neutrality seems to be the one position no one can occupy. Great suffering leads one away from God or brings us closer to him. Thus, pain is poised to become a bridge to others or a formidable barrier, a journey to greater faith or the path to despair. Scripture affirms that some suffering brings with it educational or disciplinary value: "My child, do not regard lightly the discipline of the Lord, or lose heart when you are punished by him; for the Lord disciplines those whom he loves..."(Hebrews 12:5-6). The community of Christ is filled with extraordinary people who have endured losses that stagger the imagination, yet their faith seems to burn all the brighter as time passes. With Paul they say: "[we] boast in our sufferings, knowing that suffering produces endurance, and endurance produces character, and character produces hope, and hope does not disappoint us, because God's love has been poured into our hearts through the Holy Spirit..." (Romans 5:3-5).

In my experience those richest in faith are those who have endured great pain. One friend who illustrated this for me was Kenny Barnes, a young carpenter and a fine poet whom I knew in the 1980s. Kenny and I worshiped at the same congregation, and I came to admire his poetry which celebrated the world's "ordinary mystery," as he called it. For years Kenny suffered from leukemia, undergoing repeated hospitalizations and rounds of chemotherapy. His chronic suffering taught him a deep sensitivity to the preciousness of life. In his poem "Last Days," he expresses what he did not know so well before the onset of his illness:

> They say,
>
> "These are the last days."
>
> Last days!
>
> We have always lived in our last days.
>
> Birth is a warning.[15]

In "Home After Chemotherapy," Kenny wrote, "We all come to this: / our knees." Profoundly aware of how fragile life is, how limited our bodies are, he found wonder and faith in the daily graces of small things. In the same poem he reports: "In my heart / God whispers, 'Peace.'"[16]

I do not believe that time heals all wounds (not in this life, anyway), but I do believe one can learn to carry accrued wounds with grace and resolve. Over time we discover that, yes, "The Lord is near to the broken-hearted, and saves the crushed in spirit" (Psalm 34:18). "How precious is your steadfast love, O God! All people may take refuge in the shadow of your wings!" (Psalm 36:7). Hope burns brightly because a day is coming, the biblical prophets tell us, when all wrongs will be corrected. One voice of hope was raised by Lady Julian in the fourteenth century. Though she saw the devastation of the Black Death that annihilated a third of the population of England, the more she meditated on suffering, the more certain she became of God's overwhelming love. She came to an absolute conviction that every evil would be turned to good through God's miraculous work. Sin and suffering are necessary, she wrote, *"but it is all going to be all right; it is all going to be all right; everything is going to be all right"* (my emphasis).[17]

My great problem is that I hate stumbling in the dark during the interim. I want to understand the world I live in now. On my bad days, I am like Emily Dickinson who writes that she grasps that "when Time is over" she will finally understand the mystery of suffering; still, she insistently asks, what about "That drop of Anguish / That scalds me now—that scalds me now!"[18] Yet the universe Dickinson longs for is not the one we inhabit. In this world, reality is opaque. We receive only winks, hints, nods, never "the joyful consummation."[19] Now we see through a glass darkly; and so, our choices are limited: Either we trust in the mean time or we do not; either we walk by faith or we do not.

Pilgrim hearts learn to trust where they cannot see. They join Abraham and Sarah on a faith walk. They rely on a God who teaches them to take risks, to cast their bread upon the waters, to abandon themselves, to suffer for the kingdom, to drop that seed into the soil, to let go: "Very truly, I tell you, unless a grain of wheat falls into the earth and dies, it remains just a single grain; but if it dies, it bears much fruit. Those who love their life shall lose it, and those who hate their life in this world will keep it for eternal life" (John 12:24-25). When we abandon ourselves to this unseen future, we dissolve in wonder before the majesty and mystery of our God. We yield to his compassionate touch, sustained by the promise that all shall be well, all manner of things shall be well, for "he will wipe every tear from our eyes, and death will be no more" (Revelation 21:4).

17

SEEKING: THE END
OF THE JOURNEY

Follow me.
—Jesus

Pursue love.
—Paul

Don't expect faith to clear things up for you. It is trust, not certainty...
—Flannery O'Connor

Blaise Pascal—the precocious French philosopher, scientist, mathematician, and inventor—possessed one of the greatest minds in human history. Before he was thirteen he discovered an error in Descartes's geometry. He invented the first reliable mechanical calculator (at age nineteen), the syringe, and the hydraulic press. He proved the existence of a vacuum in nature. He provided the groundwork for calculus and modern theories of probability. Most important, perhaps, he was a brilliant theologian, Christian apologist, and a humble prophet of sorts. Though devoted to science, he foresaw the terrors of a rationalism radically divorced from spiritual values. What if our love of reason causes us to forget about matters of the heart and faith? What happens if we accept the imperial claim that science can answer all questions and solve all problems?

In his famous apologetic work *Pensées*, or *Thoughts*, Pascal presents a thought experiment. Imagine a man in prison. In just one hour, he will either be pardoned or executed. If the prisoner learns within the hour that he may be executed, then he will have the power to have the sentence revoked. All he has to do is ask for a reprieve. But suppose such a man decides to play a game of cards and not bother to inquire about his status. What would you think of him? Would he be a reasonable person?[1]

Pascal conceived this anecdote in order to seize the attention of his worldly minded, careless-living friends. He offered a picture of the human condition. Time is short and the meter is running. Our fates await us. Happily, we have a say in the outcome. Yet, astonishingly, many live indifferently. They do not choose to help themselves. Card-playing is Pascal's metaphor for anyone's favorite means of diversion—the quest for pleasure, success, fame, entertainment. Human beings' infinite capacity to distract themselves from considering the ultimate questions of life was a source of wonder for Pascal.

Pascal imagines three classes of people: (1) Those who have sought God and found him; (2) those who are seeking God but have not yet found him; (3) those who are not seeking. Those in the first two categories are prudent and worthy of commendation. Those who don't even bother to look for answers are like the condemned man playing cards—they are irrational, unhappy, and without hope. He is astonished at the people who fret over trivial concerns in their lives (who slighted them, what others think of them, etc.), but who show a "strange insensitivity concerning the greatest things."[2] How can one be indifferent to one's very destiny, Pascal wonders. Either God is or he is not. Either we are immortal beings headed toward eternity or we are not. Everything hangs in the balance. "All Christianity concentrates on the man at the cross-roads....Will a man take this road or that?" says Chesterton.[3] Pascal sees it similarly. It is utterly irrational (not to say dangerous) to stand at the crossroads and not make a move.

The Bible praises those who decide to seek holy things. In the Psalms, the righteous person is the one who seeks God with all his or her heart:

"Come," my heart says, "seek his face!" Your face, Lord, do I seek. (Psalm 27:8)
God looks down from heaven on humankind to see if there are any who are wise, who seek after God. (Psalm 53:2)

> O God, you are my God, I seek you, my soul thirsts for you; my flesh faints
> for you....(Psalm 63:1)

Jesus also honors the seeker:

> Ask, and it will be given you; search, and you will find; knock, and the door
> will be opened for you. For everyone who asks receives, and everyone who
> searches finds, and for everyone who knocks, the door will be opened.
> (Matthew 7:7-8)

Throughout his ministry Jesus invited people to join the pilgrimage to life and wholeness. "Follow me," he says in the opening chapter of John's gospel (John 1:43). "Follow me," he says twice in the last chapter of the same gospel (21:19, 22). Jesus' invitation reflects how the Christian life is rather simple, at one level. It is a matter of rejecting the allure of the sedentary life in order to get out on the road and seek God. The saints through the ages can be recognized by their searching spirits. They live as strangers and foreigners on the earth. "[T]hey desire a better country, that is, a heavenly one. Therefore, God is not ashamed to be called their God; indeed, he has prepared a city for them" (Hebrews 11:14-16). A faithful heart is always a passionate pilgrim heart, ever on the road, ever moving forward—searching for understanding, seeking the face of God.

RESTORING HEART-CENTERED FAITH

"Heart" is central to Christianity. (Indeed, the word *heart* appears about 900 times in the Bible.) However, because the term has been misunderstood and abused, it has become suspect in some circles. Some even avoid the term altogether, finding in John Wesley's conversion experience ("I felt my heart strangely warmed") something hopelessly sentimental. Yet the word *heart* was often on the lips of Jesus. He treats the concept with utmost concern and respect. Indeed, for Jesus as for all the prophets, the heart of religion is religion of the heart. We must note what Jesus meant by the term.

Heart in Scripture and in the early Christian tradition is a large and essential term. In the Bible the *heart* involves thinking as well as emotion.[4] After the close of the New Testament, new, narrower definitions of the word arose—the sort one finds in romantic Valentine's Day messages or in such statements as "I followed my heart in this decision, not my head." But heart, biblically understood, does not separate intellect from feeling. The term includes multiple faculties, including the capacities to plan, think, judge, and choose. It is the zone of "emotion-fused thought," which includes intelligence, mind, wisdom, intention, will, love, sadness and joy.[5] In this light, if we love the Lord with all our heart, we are doing more than feeling generous thoughts about our Maker. We are committing our will, purposes, inclinations, thoughts, and desires to him.

According to Jesus the heart is the "true self," which God always sees (Luke 16:15). He knows our true character and nature despite what others may or may not see. Jesus was profoundly concerned about the relationship between one's "interior, innermost self and outward activity: activity flows from the heart, and it is the heart that needs realigning."[6] He saw in the religious legalists of his day a tragic fissure between inner being and outward conduct. The Pharisees were precisionists who performed certain actions by rote, but they lacked a heartfelt reverence for God (Matthew 15:8-9). Jesus also cared deeply about behavior (treating others fairly and compassionately, for example), but he expected the external forms to be congruent with, and inspired by, the interior life: "For out of the abundance of the heart the mouth speaks" (Matthew 12:34).

Recent discoveries in science are enabling us to reconsider the vital connections between thought and feeling. After centuries of segregation, some are re-imagining an integration of head and heart. According to the work of Robert and Michèle Root-Bernstein, for example, body orientation and visceral feelings play significant roles in major discoveries. Though this way of understanding has not yet made a place for "soul" or "spirit" in the biblical sense, there are signs that the Enlightenment divorce of head and heart is coming to an end.[7]

According to Scripture, it is impossible to please God without stirring and drawing upon the emotions of the heart. The Holy Spirit pours into our hearts the fire of his love (Romans 5:5). As Rowan Williams observes: "Sorrow, fear, compassion, love, delight are the very stuff of moral and spiritual life. Did not Christ experience them all fully and really?"[8] The greatest Christians through the ages (many cited in this book) demonstrate a profound unity of intellect and feeling. Passion, tears, and laughter all seem to attend the lives of the great saints. Love of God and love of our neighbor with all of our heart (and mind, soul, and strength) is our truest vocation. This is what it means to follow Jesus.

THE QUEST TO LOVE

The final scene in John's gospel defines the disciple's calling as a pilgrimage—lived out through radical love. As in many of the post-resurrection appearances, the scene is a meal, this one at sunrise. Seven of Jesus' closest followers have given up in despair after the apparent defeat at Golgotha. No longer "fishers of men," they have returned to being ordinary fisherman on the Sea of Galilee. There, we hear the voices of common laborers:

"I am going fishing."

"We will go with you."

Jesus appears, but he is not immediately recognized. On the seashore, as the sun rises above the eastern hills of Galilee, the risen Christ builds a charcoal fire and begins to cook breakfast for the disciples. Once again, the dialogue is simple and ordinary—hardly the stuff of theological reflection:

"Bring some of the fish that you have just caught."

"Come and have breakfast."

In the midst of these ordinary activities—fishing and breakfast and conversation—Jesus engages the disciples in a discussion that moves from the mundane and the particular (nets, bread, sheep, and fish—153 of them precisely) to the universal and transcendent, the very purpose of our lives upon which the destiny of the world depends. Once more we see that the eternal is rooted in the particular.

This scene depicts how vulnerable to grief and disappointment are the followers of Jesus, but it also shows that tragedy is pregnant with holy possibility, if one is alert. The danger is that we may miss the epiphany because we simply *over*look it. Quite literally we may look too high. Our upward gaze prevents our seeing that God is found in lowly places—on the floor with a basin and a towel, ready to wash our feet; at the table blessing the bread and breaking it; on the shore cooking breakfast.

We miss "the interpenetration of the holy and the mundane."[9]

In John's narrative Jesus is the one who breaks the bread and nourishes us, the one who says, "Come and have breakfast." Jesus gives life to these ordinary, discouraged workers. (Bread and fish are time-honored symbols of life; another "ordinary" meal turns sacramental.) Here we see the community of God's people in miniature. It is called into fellowship by Jesus, gathered around a common meal, feasting on his provisions, listening to his counsel, and receiving one's mission to the world. Despite the disciples' waywardness, Jesus remains faithful and forgiving. He shows up at their workplace when they had seemingly forgotten him; more, he turns to Peter, the very man who had betrayed him days before, and asks a profoundly embarrassing question: "Simon son of John, do you love me more than these?" Six other disciples solemnly look on as Peter replies, no doubt in embarrassment: "Yes, Lord; you know that I love you." Jesus speaks this penetrating question three times—perfect symmetry to balance the three vehement denials spoken on the night of Jesus' arrest.

Peter is a superb representation of every weary pilgrim who fails and falls. He is also a symbol of hope, reminding us that the Gospel is for hapless mess-ups, not perfect people. Flannery O'Connor once spoke the truth bluntly, when she said, "When we get our spiritual house in order, we'll be dead."[10] Thomas Merton is disarmingly honest about the challenges of staying true to the path:

> My Lord God, I have no idea where I am going. I do not see the road ahead of me. I cannot know for certain where it will end. Nor do I really know myself, and the fact that I think that I am following your will does not mean that I am actually doing so. But I believe that the desire to please you does in fact please you. And I hope I have that desire in all that I am doing. I hope that I will never do anything apart from that desire. And I know that if I do this you will lead me by the right road though I may know nothing about it. Therefore will I trust you always though I may seem to be lost and in the shadow of death. I will not fear, for you are ever with me, and you will never leave me to face my perils alone.[11]

I cannot help feeling that a similar spirit of humility is what attracted Jesus to Peter that morning on the seashore. It certainly wasn't his steadfast goodness.

Maybe Peter was particularly prepared for his new vocation to which Jesus was directing him because he had failed so dreadfully. "The only whole heart is a broken one," the Kotzke Rebbe once said.[12] From Peter's broken heart blossomed an extraordinary sympathy, tenderness, and humility, the very qualities of the good shepherd which Peter became in time (1 Peter 3:8). Jesus could look at the humiliated man before him and see the strong, courageous, humble pastor—and faithful martyr—that he would become thirty years later. In time Peter became his Lord's vision, an agent of grace to the world.

Jesus continues to place his trust in people like Peter—like us—who do not measure up. What is required is not perfection but a willingness to love. Without love, there is no healing or life. Loving others is the supreme spiritual practice. When Jesus says, "This is my commandment, that you love one another as I have loved you" (John 15:12), he points us to a love that touches real lives, real bodies. It transforms human relationship: "Love is patient; love is kind; love is not envious or boastful or arrogant or rude. It does not insist on its own way; it is not irritable or resentful; it does not rejoice in wrongdoing, but rejoices in the truth. It bears all things, believes all things, hopes all things, endures all things" (1 Corinthians 13:4-7). This then is the way of Jesus in everyday life: to live a life of gift-giving love towards everyone we meet. To say "How wonderful that you exist!"[13] To say with Hopkins, Christ lies in and "under the world's splendour and wonder."[14] This is not an easy road or a short one. In time, though, something wonderfully mysterious happens. Christ appears in the face of the faithful pilgrim who stays on the Way.

Bob Keeshan, known to millions as Captain Kangaroo, was for decades the beloved host of a morning television show for children. When he began his role as the grandfatherly Captain in 1955, Keeshan was only twenty-eight years old; and so, to look the part, he had to wear a great deal of make-up, fake whiskers, and a wig. But as he played the role through the years, his hair turned white and wrinkles appeared. Keeshan found that he needed less and less make-up. Near the end of his career he could say: *"I have grown into the part."*[15] Exactly.

The pilgrim heart will, in time, be shaped in the image of Christ. Initially, the likeness will be faint, hardly plausible at all. But if we walk the road with him, loving as he taught us, then we *become* what we perform in due time. "It is no longer I who live, but it is Christ who lives in me" (Galatians 2:20). At first we speak these words as a hopeful prayer; one day they will be true. Many Christians today do not understand that conversion is progressive. Westerhoff and Eusden note:

> No aspect of thinking on conversion is more foreign to the American evangelical experience than this stress on conversion as a process.... Evangelicals emphasize emotion and an initial movement. This moment is celebrated, recalled, and when the experience fades, recaptured. But Christian tradition does not agree....Conversion is a continuous and lifelong process. Conversions proceed layer by layer, relationship by relationship, here a little, there a little—until the whole personality, intellect, feeling, and will have been recreated by God.[16]

We are *changed* (Paul employs a Greek word which is the root of the English word *metamorphosis*) into the divine image incrementally, step by step, "from one degree of glory to another" (2 Corinthians 3:18). Furthermore, it occurs through the Holy Spirit's powerful work in our lives, not through our effort or ingenuity. These two facts lead to patience (for the transformation requires much time, trial, error, pain, and failure) and humility (since it is never our doing; we are recipients of a holy gift).

Sometimes the journey to Christlikeness looks simple and easy enough. It may involve cooking breakfast for someone, or washing their feet, giving them a lift, reading them a book, or repairing their plumbing. (Though even these, I suspect, can be hard assignments when they interrupt our carefully laid-out plans.) Others may cost us a great deal. The Master gave Peter a stark warning. Following Jesus will cost the Apostle his life:

> Very truly, I tell you, when you were younger, you used to fasten your own belt and go wherever you wished. But when you grow old, you will stretch out your hands, and someone else will fasten a belt around you and take you where you do not wish to go. (He said this to indicate the kind of death by which he would glorify God.) (John 21:18-19)

However great or small, each act of service we do costs something. Together these deeds of care meld, like the colors of the spectrum, into the pure white light of gift-giving love. The commandments are subsumed under one great principle—love—as the Apostle teaches: "Owe no one anything, except to love one another; for the one who loves another has fulfilled the law....Love does no wrong to a neighbor; therefore, love is the fulfilling of the law" (Romans 13:8, 10). Lady Julian spent many years reflecting on the purpose of the Christian life. Why are we here? To what end? After fifteen years of ceaseless prayer and reflection, she came to this final insight:

> Would you know our Lord's meaning in all this? Learn it well. Love was the meaning. Who showed it to you? Love. Why did God show it to you? For love. Hold fast to this and you shall learn and know more about love. But you shall never learn anything except love from God. So I was taught that love was our Lord's meaning. And I saw full surely that before ever God made us, God loved us. This love was never quenched nor ever shall be. And in this love God created everything that is. And in this love God has made all things for our benefit. In this love is our life everlasting. All this shall we see in God without end—which Christ grant us. Amen.[17]

In the end, the followers of Jesus know only love. We were created in love in order to love, so that we may finally be embraced forever by a greater Love that will never let us go. This is the way of the pilgrim heart.

NOTES

INTRODUCTION:

AN INVITATION TO BEGIN AGAIN

1 Throughout the book I use the term *saint* in its original New Testament sense, that is, a follower of Jesus, a person striving to live a holy life, a member of the Christian community (see 1 Corinthians 1:2, Acts 9:32 etc.). I do not use the term in its specialized, post-biblical sense of an "exceptionally holy" person who has been recognized for "sainthood" by a particular religious communion. Despite the possible confusion, I use the word advisedly. It is a fine biblical term whose original meaning deserves restoration.

2 Colossians 1:27; Romans 8:29; 2 Corinthians 3:17-18.

3 C. S. Lewis, *Mere Christianity* (New York: Macmillan, 1966): 65.

4 Charles Williams, *The Descent of the Dove: A Short History of the Holy Spirit in the Church* (London: Religious Book Club, 1939): 83.

5 See, for example: Richard Foster, *Celebration of Discipline* (San Francisco: Harper and Row, 1988); Rodney Clapp, *Tortured Wonders: Christian Spirituality for People, Not Angels* (Grand Rapids, MI: Brazos, 2004); Dallas Willard, *The Spirit of the Disciplines* (San Francisco: Harper & Row, 1988); Robert Barron, *The Strangest Way: Walking the Christian Path* (Maryknoll, NY: Orbis, 2004); Marjorie J. Thompson, *Soul Feast: An Invitation to the Christian Spiritual Life* (Louisville: Westminster/John Knox, 1995); Dorothy Bass, *Practicing Our Faith: A Way of Life for a Searching People* (San Franciso: Jossey-Bass, 1997); Gary Holloway and Earl Lavender, *Living God's Love: An Invitation to Christian Spirituality* (Siloam Springs, AR: Leafwood, 2004); Luke Timothy Johnson, *Living Jesus: Learning the Heart of the Gospel* (San Francisco: HarperSanFranciso, 1999); Stephanie Paulsell, *Honoring the Body: Meditations on a Christian Practice* (San Francisco: Jossey-Bass, 2002); Samuel M. Powell and Michael E. Lodahl, eds., *Embodied Holiness: Toward a Corporate Theology of Spiritual Growth* (Downers Grove, IL: InterVarsity, 1999); Robert E. Webber, *Ancient-Future Faith: Rethinking Evangelicalism for a Postmodern World* (Grand Rapids: Baker, 1999); Miroslav Volf and Dorothy C. Bass, eds., *Practicing Theology: Beliefs and Practices in the Christian Life* (Grand Rapids: Eerdmans, 2002); N. T. Wright, *Following Jesus: Biblical Reflections on Discipleship* (Grand Rapids: Eerdmans, 1994); Ray S. Anderson, *The Shape of Practical Theology* (Downers Grove, IL: InterVarsity, 2001).

6 See, for example: Philip Jenkins, *The Next Christendom: The Coming of Global Christianity* (Oxford: Oxford University Press, 2002); and Brian McLaren, *A Generous Orthodoxy* (Grand Rapids: Zondervan, 2004).

CHAPTER 1:
THE CALL TO A 'WORLDLY' SPIRITUALITY

1 I am grateful to Roger Lundin for his hypothesis on Emily Dickinson's Gnostic tendencies. See his *Emily Dickinson and the Art of Belief* (Grand Rapids: Eerdmans, 2004). The phrase "emotional seclusion" is Professor Lundin's (80).

2 Emily Dickinson, Letter to James D. Clark, Autumn 1882; *Selected Poems and Letters of Emily Dickinson*, ed. Robert N. Linscott (New York: Doubleday, 1959): 320.

3 Lundin 203.

4 Gnosticism appears in many different forms, and so cannot be easily defined or classified. In the second century of the Christian era it posed a threat to the faith by denying the spiritual value of creation and the human body, therefore, denying the possibility of redemption through Christ's physical death and bodily resurrection. It was "a flight from the particular.... God and the world are strangers to one another; that there is a world is the result of accident or malevolence on the part of some heavenly power. Thus the historical and temporal order...is in no way within the purposes of God; it is an abortion, a calamity," writes Rowan Williams. According to this system of thought, Williams explains, human souls are imprisoned in the body, and they "must be released to return to their home in God....thus the religious impetus of Gnosticism is the longing to escape from the temporal and the fleshly." See Williams's *The Wound of Knowledge* (Cambridge, MA: Cowley, 1990): 34. Gnostic tendencies appear in various Christian and non-Christian heresies through the centuries, including in the New Age movement today. Dickinson's Gnostic dualism may be seen in her exalting the soul over the body. While she does not reject material creation like the Gnostics, she does find the world to be a "magic prison" from which the soul escapes.

5 Linscott 239.

6 Linscott 320. The number of poems in which Dickinson declares her preference for spirit over matter is considerable. Consider "Of all the souls that stand create," in which she imagines the afterlife as a place where souls stand apart from "this brief tragedy of flesh," and where her love of one soul trumps all of the material universe: "Behold the atom I preferred / To all the lists of clay!"

7 Isolation from community was a frequent theme in Dickinson's poetry. In one poem ("I'm ceded—I've stopped being Theirs—") she describes her putting away her childhood faith, in the same way she puts away her dolls. She trades Christian community for the imperial self. See Lundin 48-61.

8 Miroslav Volf, "Theology for a Way of Life," *Practicing Theology: Beliefs and Practices in Christian Life*, eds. Miroslav Volf and Dorothy C. Bass (Grand Rapids: Eerdmans, 2002): 256.

9 Stanley Hauerwas, "The Sanctified Body: Why Perfection Does Not Require a 'Self,'" in *Embodied Holiness: Toward a Corporate Theology of Spiritual Growth*, eds. Samuel M. Powell and Michael E. Lodahl (Downers Grove, IL: Intervarsity, 1999): 21-22.

10 For an extended discussion of the biblical meaning of the word "heart," see Chapter 17.

11 Acts 9:2; 18:25, 26; 19:9, 23; 22:4; 24:14; 25:3.

12 *Apophthegmata*, Anonymous Supplements. Quoted in Bernard McGinn et al., *Christian Spirituality: Origins to the Twelfth Century* (New York: Crossroad, 1987): 407.

CHAPTER 2:

THE BLESSING OF BODY AND SOUL

1 Marilynne Robinson, *Gilead* (New York: Farrar, Straus, Giroux, 1994): 69-70.

2 The heresy is Manichaeism, a form of dualism that holds that matter is evil. Thomas Merton warns against "a kind of Manichean attitude toward natural beauty on the one hand, and a rationalistic neglect of sensible things on the other" which leads the worshiper to abandon "the normal culture of the senses, of artistic taste, of imagination, and of intelligence...." *Contemplative Prayer* (New York: Image, 1971): 84-85.

3 Meister Eckhart, *Breakthrough: Meister Eckhart's Creation Spirituality in New Translation* (Garden City, NY: Image Books, 1980): 131. Cultists like the Heaven's Gate followers vigorously assert the separateness of body and spirit. For these, the body is merely a "suit of clothes" that can be easily discarded so as to allow the true self, the spirit, to fly free. Unfortunately, many Christians think in similar terms.

4 Stanley Hauerwas, "The Sanctified Body: Why Perfection Does Not Require a 'Self,'" in *Embodied Holiness: Toward a Corporate Theology of Spiritual Growth*, eds. Samuel M. Powell and Michael E. Lodahl (Downers Grove, IL: Intervarsity, 1999): 23-24.

5 Dietrich Bonhoeffer, *Letters and Papers from Prison* (London: Collins, 1960): 56.

6 See Miroslav Volf, "Theology for a Way of Life," *Practicing Theology: Beliefs and Practices in Christian Life*, eds. Miroslav Volf and Dorothy C. Bass (Grand Rapids: Eerdmans, 2002): 255-260.

7 Robinson 69-70.

8 Czeslaw Milosz, "Either—Or," *New and Collected Poems, 1931-2001* (New York: HarperCollins, 2001): 540.

9 Hauerwas 29.

10 Luke Timothy Johnson, *Living Jesus: Learning the Heart of the Gospel* (San Francisco: HarperSanFrancisco, 1999).

11 Richard Foster, *Prayer: Finding the Heart's True Home* (San Francisco: HarperSanFrancisco, 1992): 171.

12 Nicholas Herman of Lorraine, *The Practice of the Presence of God* (White Plains, NY: Peter Pauper, 1963): 25.

CHAPTER 3:

EMPTYING: A FRESH BREEZE AS WE LET GO

1 George F. R. Ellis, "Kenosis as a Unifying Theme for Life and Cosmology," Polkinghorne, ed., *The Work of Love: Creation as Kenosis* (Grand Rapids, MI: Eerdmans, 2001): 108.

2 For a thoughtful study of *kenosis* in creation, see John Polkinghorne, ed., *Work of Love*. While a Darwinian model argues that there is no altruism in nature, but only a brutal self-interest in survival at the expense of all other creatures, new understandings of interdependence and symbiosis in ecological systems suggest a kind of *kenosis* in creation. See also Polkinghorne, *Science and the Trinity: The Christian Encounter with Reality* (New Haven: Yale University Press, 2004).

3 Dietrich Bonhoeffer, *The Cost of Discipleship* (New York: Macmillan, 1963): 98-99.

4 Simone Weil, *Waiting for God* (New York: Harper and Row, 1951): 194-195.

5 See, for example: Henri Nouwen, *The Road to Daybreak: A Spiritual Journey* (New York: Doubleday/Image, 1990); Nouwen, *In the Name of Jesus: Reflections on Christian Leadership* (New York: Crossroad, 1989).

6 Nouwen, *Road to Daybreak* 154.

7 Walt McDonald, *Blessings the Body Gave* (Columbus: Ohio State University Press, 1998): 29.

8 Robert Bellah, *Beyond Belief: Essays on Religion in a Post-Traditional World* (New York: Harper and Row, 1976): xx-xxi.

9 Nouwen, *In the Name of Jesus* 59.

10 Miroslav Volf, *Exclusion and Embrace: A Theological Exploration of Identity, Otherness, and Reconciliation* (Nashville: Abingdon, 1996): 25-26.

Chapter 4:

Welcoming: Opening Doors to Strangers

1 Christine Pohl, *Making Room: Recovering Hospitality as a Christian Tradition* (Grand Rapids: Eerdmans, 1999): 44-45.

2 Rodney Stark, *The Rise of Christianity* (San Francisco: HarperSanFrancisco, 1996): 73-94.

3 See, for example: Christine Pohl, *Making Room*; and Rodney Stark, *The Rise of Christianity*.

4 Stark 77; William H. McNeill, *Plagues and Peoples* (Garden City, NY: Doubleday, 1976); Arthur E. R. Boak, *A History of Rome to 565 A.D.*, 3rd ed. (New York: Macmillan, 1947).

5 Stark 82.

6 Tertullian, *Apology* 39.

7 Pohl 108. Basil also established a hospital in Caesarea in approximately A.D. 370 (Pohl 44).

8 Stark, 161.

9 Pohl 45.

10 Basil, quoted in *An Advent Sourcebook,* ed. Thomas J. O'Gorman (Chicago: Archdiocese of Chicago, 1988): 45.

11 According to James D. G. Dunn, in the New Testament *abba* conveys the idea of courtesy, respect, and "childlike confidence and obedience." See Dunn's *Jesus and the Spirit* (Grand Rapids: Eerdmans, 1997): 22.

12 Henri Nouwen, *Reaching Out: The Three Movements of the Spiritual Life* (Garden City, NY: Doubleday, 1966): 55.

13 Nouwen, *Life of the Beloved: Spiritual Living in a Secular World* (New York: Crossroad, 1992): 85, 87.

Chapter 5

Resting: The Day Sabbath Becomes Joy

1 See Joe Rao, "Disappearing Stars: How 2,500 Points of Light have Dwindled to 15," SPACE.com 21 Mar. 2002 http://www.space.com/spacewatch/light_pollution_030321.html; Joan Lowy, "Light Pollution Obscures the Stars," *Abilene Reporter-News* 13 Jan. 2002: 6A.

2 See "New Research Shows Artificial Light at Night Stimulates Breast Cancer Growth in

Laboratory Mice." *NIH News* 19 Dec 2005. http://www.nih.gov/news/pr/dec2005/niehs-19.htm.

3 Tilden Edwards explains that Christians have developed two somewhat different understandings of sabbath—sabbath as "festival" (a joyous celebration) and Sabbath as a "fast" (pleasure-denying), the former promoted by Anglicans and Roman Catholics, the latter emphasized by the Puritan Reformers, especially in England and America. The latter, "sabbatarianism," sought to suppress all forms of amusement on Sunday. See Tilden Edwards, *Sabbath Time* (Nashville: Upper Room, 1992): 28-29.

4 A. N. Wilson, *How Can We Know?* (New York: Atheneum, 1985): 11.

5 Thomas Merton, quoted in John Michael Talbot, *The Lessons of St. Francis* (New York: Penguin, 1998): 59, 63.

6 Merton, *New Seeds of Contemplation* (New York: New Directions, 1961): 53.

7 Merton 55.

8 Merton 57.

9 Darryl Tippens, "Loneliness and Community: An Interview with Henri Nouwen," *Wineskins* 2.7: 14-19.

10 Henri Nouwen, *Adam: God's Beloved* (Maryknoll, NY: Orbis, 1997): 54.

11 Herbert Wright Gates, *Recreation and the Church* (Chicago: University of Chicago, 1917): 10-12, 19.

12 Josef Pieper, "Leisure as a Spiritual Attitude," *Weavings* 8 Mar.-Apr. 1993: 6-12.

Chapter 6

Resting: More Sabbath Blessings

1 Dorothy C. Bass, *Receiving the Day: Christian Practices for Opening the Gift of Time* (San Francisco: Jossey-Bass, 2000): 59.

2 Steven Sample, *The Contrarian's Guide to Leadership* (San Francisco: Jossey-Bass, 2002): 167, 168.

3 See John Ortberg, "Taking Care of Busyness," *Leadership* Fall 1998: 30.

4 "Guerrilla compassion" is the name for Sharon Salzburg's practice of silently blessing people standing in lines at banks and supermarkets and people in cars stuck in traffic. See Wayne Muller, *Sabbath: Finding Rest, Renewal, and Delight in Our Busy Lives* (New York: Bantam, 2000): 46.

5 Mary Pipher, *The Shelter of Each Other: Rebuilding Our Families* (New York: Grosset / Putnam, 1996): 12-13.

6 Richard Foster, *Freedom of Simplicity* (San Francisco: Harper and Row, 1981): 78-79.

7 Lady Julian, quoted in *Westminster Collection of Christian Quotations*, ed. Martin H. Manser (Louisville: Westminster John Knox, 2001): 362.

8 A traditional tale cited in Muller 48.

CHAPTER 7

BEFRIENDING: THE MUTUAL REGARD AND CARE OF SOULS

1 Horace, quoted in Michel de Montaigne, *The Complete Essays*, trans. M. A. Screech (London: Penguin, 1991): 217. *Satires*, I.v.44.

2 See John 19:26; 20:2; 21:7, 20.

3 Augustine, *Confessions*, trans. Henry Chadwick (Oxford: Oxford University Press, 1992): 160 (IX.iv.7).

4 Augustine, *Confessions* 59 (IV.vi.11).

5 Aelred of Rievaulx, *Spiritual Friendship* (Kalamazoo, MI: Cistercian Pub., Inc., 1977); "On Affectionate Relationships" in Montaigne 205-19.

6 See, for example: C.S.Lewis, *The Four Loves* (San Diego: Harcourt, Brace, Jovanovich, 1960); David G. Brenner, *Sacred Companions: The Gift of Spiritual Friendship and Direction* (Downers Grove, IL: InterVarsity, 2002); Martin Marty, *Friendship* (Allen, TX: Argus, 1980); Eugene Kennedy, *On Being a Friend* (New York: Ballantine, 1982).

7 Lewis 87.

8 Larry B. Stammer, "Promises Can't Keep Stadiums Packed Forever," *Los Angeles Times* 2 Jul. 2005: B2.

9 Esther de Waal, *The Celtic Way of Prayer: The Recovery of the Religious Imagination* (New York: Doubleday, 1997): 135.

10 de Waal 135-136.

11 de Waal 137.

12 David K. Lewis, Carley Dodd, and Darryl Tippens, *The Gospel According to Generation X: The Culture of Adolescent Faith* (Abilene, TX: Abilene Christian University Press, 1995): 73-85.

13 Joseph Heller, *Good as Gold* (New York: Simon and Schuster, 1979): 426-427.

14 Marty 11.

15 William Shakespeare, *Merchant of Venice* 3.4.12.

16 *Confessions* 59 (IV.vii).

17 Erich Fromm, T*he Art of Loving* (New York: Harper and Row, 1974): 46.

18 Rilke, quoted in Marty 102.

19 Marty, *Friendship*, 129.

20 Simone Weil, *Waiting for God* (New York: Harper and Row, 1951): 204.

21 Marty 117.

22 Aelred of Rievaulx, "On Spiritual Friendship," *The Literature of Medieval England*, ed. D. W. Robertson (New York: McGraw-Hill, 1970): 21.

23 Robert Browning, "Paracelsus," *The Complete Works of Robert Browning*, ed. Roma A. King, Jr. (Athens: Ohio University Press, 1969): 98.

24 Stuart Miller, *Men and Friendship* (Los Angeles: Jeremy P. Tarcher, Inc., 1992): 9.

25 Weil 93, 200.

26 Aelred, *Spiritual Friendship* 51.

27 Lewis, *Four Loves* 111.

CHAPTER 8
CONFESSING: I SWEAR TO TELL THE WHOLE TRUTH

1 Dietrich Bonhoeffer, *Life Together*, trans. John W. Doberstein (New York: Harper & Row, 1954): 110.

2 Donald Miller, *Blue Like Jazz* (Nashville: Thomas Nelson, 2003): 117.

3 Miller 118.

4 Miller 118.

5 Miller 123.

6 Miller 125.

7 Bonhoeffer, *Life Together* 112, 114.

8 Bonhoeffer, *Life Together* 112.

9 See, for example: Margaret Guenther, *Holy Listening: The Art of Spiritual Direction* (Boston: Cowley, 1992); Larry Crabb, *Connecting: Healing Ourselves and Our Relationships, A Radical New Vision* (Nashville: Word, 1997).

10 Richard Foster, *Prayer: Finding the Heart's True Home* (San Francisco: HarperSanFrancisco, 1992): 27-35.

11 *The Book of Common Prayer* (New York: Oxford University Press, 1990).

12 Foster, *Prayer* 224.

CHAPTER 9
FORGIVING: THE LOVE THAT TRAVELS FARTHER

1 Duane W. H. Arnold, ed. and trans., *Prayers of the Martyrs* (Grand Rapids: Zondervan, 1991): 108-109.

2 Arnold 74.

3 Arnold 70.

4 Miroslav Volf, *Exclusion and Embrace: A Theological Exploration of Identity, Otherness, and Reconciliation* (Nashville: Abingdon, 1996): 126.

5 Rowan Williams, "Barth on the Triune God," *Karl Barth: Studies of His Theological Method*, ed. S.W. Sykes (Oxford, Oxford University Press, 1979): 177.

6 Jürgen Moltmann, quoted in Volf 122.

7 Ira Byock, *The Four Things That Matter Most* (New York: Free Press, 2004): 3.

8 Byock 40.

9 Dietrich Bonhoeffer, *The Cost of Discipleship* (New York: Macmillan, 1963): 118-119.

10 C. S. Lewis, *Prayer: Letters to Malcolm* (London: HarperCollins, 1998): 95.

11 Frederick Buechner, *Telling Secrets* (New York: HarperSanFrancisco, 1991): 38.

12 Buechner 31.

13 Buechner 33.

14 "The Revenge of Truth." "Isak Dinesen [Karen Blixen]," *European Writers*, vol. 10 (New York: Scribner, 1983-1991): 1301.

15 Lewis B. Smedes, *Forgive and Forget: Healing the Hurts You Don't Deserve* (San Francisco: Harper and Row, 1984): 72.

16 Smedes 72.

17 Horton Foote, *Horton Foote: Four New Plays* (Newberry, VT: Smith and Kraus, 1993): 61.

18 See, for example: Lewis B. Smedes, *Forgive and Forget*; Richard W. Rouse, *Fire of Grace: The Healing Power of Forgiveness* (Minneapolis: Augsburg, 2005); Solomon Schimmel, *Wounds Not Healed by Time: The Power of Repentance and Forgiveness* (Oxford: Oxford University Press, 2002); Doris Donnelly, *Learning to Forgive* (New York: Macmillan, 1979); Miroslav Volf, *Free of Charge: Giving and Forgiving in a Culture Stripped of Grace* (Grand Rapids: Zondervan, 2005).

19 Reinhold Niebuhr, quoted in Smedes 132.

CHAPTER 10

LISTENING: WITHIN THE DEEP STREAM OF SILENCE

1 Thomas Merton, *New Seeds of Contemplation* (New York: New Directions, 1961): 55.

2 C. S. Lewis, *Prayer: Letters to Malcolm* (London: HarperCollins, 1998): 72.

3 Søren Kierkegaard, in *The Oxford Book of Prayer*, ed. George Appleton (Oxford: Oxford University Press, 1987): 259.

4 Raymond Carpentier, quoted in André Neher, *The Exile of the Word: From the Silence of the Bible to the Silence of Auschwitz* (Philadelphia: Jewish Publication Society of America, 1981): 48-49.

5 Merton 55.

6 Merton 53.

7 Henri Nouwen, "Moving from Solitude to Community to Ministry," *Leadership* Spring 1995: 82.

8 Nouwen, "Moving from Solitude" 81-82.

9 Other suggestions: George Appleton, ed., *The Oxford Book of Prayer* (Oxford: Oxford University Press, 1987); Michael Counsell, ed., *2000 Years of Prayer* (Harrisburg, PA: Morehouse, 1999); Leonard Allen, ed., *The Contemporaries Meet the Classics on Prayer* (West Monroe, LA: Howard Pub. Co., 2003).

10 Consider: Richard Foster, *The Celebration of Discipline* (San Francisco: Harper & Row, 1988); Marjorie Thompson, *Soul Feast: An Invitation to the Christian Spiritual Life* (Louisville: Westminster John Knox, 1995); Alister E. McGrath, *Christian Spirituality* (Oxford: Blackwell, 1999); Dallas Willard, *The Spirit of the Disciplines* (San Francisco: Harper & Row, 1988); Eugene Peterson, *Christ Plays in Ten Thousand Places* (Grand Rapids: Eerdmans, 2005).

11 Nouwen, "Moving from Solitude" 83.

12 Simone Weil, *Waiting for God* (New York: Harper and Row, 1951): 195.

CHAPTER 11

DISCERNING: THE GIFT OF WISDOM

1 Søren Kierkegaard's *Journals and Papers*, vol. 5: Autobiographical: Part One, eds. and trans., Howard V. Hong and Edna H. Hong (Bloomington: Indiana University Press, 1978): 34-35.

2 William Shakespeare, *1 Henry IV*, Part One 5.2.102.

3 Parker Palmer, *Let Your Life Speak: Listening for the Voice of Vocation* (San Francisco: Jossey-Bass, 2000): 10.

4 Salman Rushdie, "Books vs. Goons" ["The Power of the Pen: Does Writing Change

Anything?"], *Los Angeles Times* 24 Apr. 2005: M1, 3.

5 The writer of Proverbs associates wisdom and insight with "fear of the Lord," knowledge of God, and keeping the commandments (Proverbs 4:4-7; 9:10).

6 Gregory the Great, *Homilies on Ezekiel 7.1.8*, quoted in Bernard McGinn and John Meyendorff, *Christian Spirituality: Origins to the Twelfth Century* (New York: Crossroad, 1987): 420. Luke Timothy Johnson calls for "an ecclesial hermeneutic," that is, a way of reading the Bible that is developed by, in, and through the community called the church. *Scripture and Discernment: Decision Making in the Church* (Nashville: Abingdon, 1996).

7 See Alan Jacobs, *Theology of Reading: The Hermeneutics of Love* (Boulder, CO: Westview, 2001); Fritz Oehlschlaeger, *Love and Good Reasons: Postliberal Approaches to Christian Ethics and Literature* (Durham, NC: Duke University Press, 1993): 9-48; George Steiner, *Real Presences* (Chicago: University of Chicago Press, 1991): 155-158.

8 Flannery O'Connor, *The Habit of Being: Letters of Flannery O'Connor*, ed. Sally Fitzgerald (New York: Farrar Straus Giroux, 1988): 476-477.

9 Douglas Groothius, "What Would Jesus Think?" *Chronicle of Higher Education* 4 October 2003: B14.

10 See Chapter 17 for a discussion of the biblical meaning of "heart."

11 Blaise Pascal, *Selections from the Thoughts*, ed. and trans. Arthur H. Beattie (Arlington Heights, IL: AHM, 1965): 70, 98. Thoughts # 267 and 288.

12 Robert Sternberg, ed., *Why Smart People Can Be So Stupid* (New Haven: Yale University Press, 2002).

13 T. S. Eliot, Choruses from "The Rock," *The Complete Poems and Plays 1909-1950* (New York: Harcourt, Brace and World, 1962): 96.

14 Pascal 98. Thought # 288.

15 Luke Timothy Johnson's *Scripture and Discernment: Decision Making in the Church* (Nashville: Abingdon, 1996) provides an extensive analysis of how decision-making occurred in early Christianity and suggests how it might operate in churches today, with Acts 15 as a particularly important example.

16 Henri Nouwen, *The Road to Daybreak: A Spiritual Journey* (New York: Doubleday / Image, 1990): 154.

17 Suzanne G. Farnham, et al., *Listening Hearts: Discerning Call in Community*, rev. ed. (Harrisburg, PA: Morehouse, 1991): 36-37.

18 See Daniel Taylor, *The Myth of Certainty: The Reflective Christian and the Risk of Commitment* (Downers Grove, IL: InterVarsity, 1992).

19 Kierkegaard, *Journals and Papers* 35, 37.

20 In the Book of Proverbs, wisdom is personified as someone who seeks us, but whom we ignore: "...I have called you and you refused, have stretched out my hand and no one heeded..." (Proverbs 1:24).

CHAPTER 12

SINGING: THE WAY TO HEAVEN'S DOOR

1 Anne Lamott, *Traveling Mercies: Some Thoughts on Faith* (New York: Pantheon, 1999): 48.

2 Lamott 50.

3 Lamott 47.

4 Robert Wuthnow shows that the arts, music in particular, are at the center of a revival of

American Christianity. See *All in Sync: How Music and Art Are Revitalizing American Religion* (Berkeley: University of California Press, 2003).

5 Augustine, *Confessions*, trans. Henry Chadwick (Oxford: Oxford University Press, 1992): 164 (IX.vi.14).

6 Kathleen Norris, *Cloister Walk* (New York, Riverhead Books): 90.

7 His poem "Church Music" contains these lines: "Sweetest of sweets, I thank you: when displeasure / Did through my body wound my mind, / You took me thence, and in your house of pleasure / A dainty lodging me assigned....But if I travel in your company, You know the way to heaven's door." Louis Martz, ed., *George Herbert and Henry Vaughan* (Oxford: Oxford University Press, 1986): 56-57.

8 Matt Redman, *Facedown* (Ventura, CA: Regal / Gospel Light, 2004): 23-24.

9 Dietrich Bonhoeffer once exposed the false piety of Christians who are uncomfortable with the passionate nature of the Psalter, "in so doing they want to be even more spiritual than God is...." *Life Together; Prayerbook of the Bible*, eds. Gerhard Muller and Albrecht Schönherr, trans. Daniel W. Bloesch and James H. Burtness (Minneapolis: Fortress, 1996): 168.

10 Wuthnow 179.

11 Don E. Saliers, "Singing Our Lives," in *Practicing Our Faith*, ed. Dorothy C. Bass (San Francisco: Jossey-Bass, 1997): 183.

12 Saliers, "Singing Our Lives" 192.

13 "[P]erhaps our prayer (worship) determines our belief (theology) more than our belief (theology) determines our prayer (worship)." C. Randall Bradley, "Congregational Song as Shaper of Theology: A Contemporary Assessment" *Review and Expositor* 100 (Summer 2003): 357.

14 According to Wuthnow's survey, 61% of the public says that listening to music has been important "in helping them grow spiritually and to develop a closer relationship with God"(69).

15 Bradley 357.

16 Saliers, *Worship as Theology: Foretaste of Glory Divine* (Nashville: Abingdon, 1994): 15.

17 James Baldwin, "Sonny's Blues," *Classics of Modern Fiction: Twelve Short Novels*, ed. Irving Howe, 4th ed. (San Diego: Harcourt Brace Jovanovich, 1986): 634.

18 Baldwin 642.

19 J. Nathan Corbitt quoted in Bradley 365.

20 Jan Swafford, *Charles Ives: A Life in Music* (New York: W.W. Norton, 1996): 88.

21 Wuthnow 70-71.

22 Milton, "Il Penseroso," lines 163-166.

Chapter 13

Creating: The Truth of Beauty

1 *The Inferno of Dante*, trans. Probert Pinsky (New York: Farrar, Straus and Giroux, 1994): 41-43.

2 Robert Wuthnow, *All in Sync: How Music and Art Are Revitalizing American Religion* (Berkeley: University of California Press, 2003). See especially Chapter 3 "A Blending of Cultures: The Arts and Spirituality" and Chapter 4 "Personal Spirituality: Art and the Practice of Spiritual Discipline."

3 Paulinus of Nola, *Ancient Christian Writers*, *The Poems of Paulinus of Nola*, ed. and trans. P.

G. Walsh (New York: Newman Press, 1975): 273.

4 The Greek word *poema* (giving us the modern English word "poem") signifies "work of art" or "handiwork."

5 The New Testament calls Jesus a tekton, not just a "carpenter" but an "artificer," that is, a craftsman, or a skilled, artistic worker.

6 Madeleine L'Engle wrote: "Jesus was not a theologian. He was God who told stories." *Walking on Water: Reflections on Faith & Art* (Wheaton, Ill.: Harold Shaw, 1980): 54. "Theology is actually poetry, poetry concerning God," Petrarch once said.

7 T. S. Eliot, *Murder in the Cathedral* (San Diego: Harcourt Brace Jovanovich, 1963): 70.

8 Bernard Häring, *Free and Faithful in Christ*, vol. 2 (New York: Seasbury Press, 1979): 102.

9 Häring 102.

10 Gregory of Nyssa makes this helpful distinction between living in the flesh and living after the flesh. See *The Fathers of the Church, Gregory of Nyssa, Ascetical Works*, trans. Virginia Woods Callahan (Washington: Catholic University of America Press, 1967): 110-111.

11 Augustine, *Confessions*, trans. Henry Chadwick (Oxford: Oxford University Press, 1992): 289 (XIII.xx.28).

12 "He shines in all that's fair" is a line from "This Is My Father's World." Arthur F. Holmes's book is *All Truth Is God's Truth* (Grand Rapids: Eerdmans, 1977).

13 Joseph Sittler, *Gravity and Grace: Reflections and Provocations*, ed. Linda-Marie Delloff (Minneapolis: Ausburg, 1986): 95.

14 For an excellent discussion of how to "read" contemporary film theologically, see Robert K. Johnston, *Reel Spirituality: Theology and Film in Dialogue*, 2nd ed. (Grand Rapids: Baker Academic, 2007).

15 Thomas Aquinas, *Summa Theologiae*, vol. 2, *Existence and Nature of God* (1a-2-11), ed. and trans. Timothy McDermott (London: Oxford University Press, 1964): 71, 73.

16 C. S. Lewis, *Surprised by Joy: The Shape of My Early Life* (San Diego: Harcourt Brace, 1955): 78.

17 Simone Weil, *Waiting for God* (New York: Harper and Row, 1951): 165, 172.

18 L'Engle 50.

19 Czeslaw Milosz quoted in Mary Rourke and Jon Thurber, "Czeslaw Milosz, 93: Nobel-Winning Laureate Confronted Torments of His Era," *Los Angeles Times* 15 Aug. 2004: B14.

20 Emil Brunner, *The Divine Imperative, A Study in Christain Ehics*, trans. Olive Wyon (London: Lutterworth, 1937): 499.

21 Weil 162.

22 Many are noting the current outpouring of new Christian music. Robert Wutnnow documents the revival of interest in the arts in churches. See *All in Sync: How Music and Art Are Revitalizing American Religion*.

23 Thiessen 338.

CHAPTER 14

FEASTING: MEMORY AND MEALTIMES

1 Augustine, *Confessions*, trans. Henry Chadwick (Oxford: Oxford University Press, 1992): 244 (XI.xxix.39).

2 Walter Brueggemann, *Texts Under Negotiation: The Bible and Postmodern Imagination* (Minneapolis: Fortress, 1993): 55.

3 Augustine, *Confessions* 186-187 (X.vii.14).

4 William Katerberg, "History, Hope, and the Redemption of Time," *The Future of Hope: Christian Tradition amid Modernity and Postmodernity*, eds., Miroslav Volf and William Katerberg (Grand Rapids: Eerdmans, 2004): 73.

5 Wilken, "Tradition and Trust: The Role of Memory in the Christian Intellectual Tradition," Gregory Wolfe, ed., *The New Religious Humanists: A Reader* (New York: Free Press, 1997): 58.

6 Brueggemann 39.

7 Katerberg argues, with Hans-Georg Gadamer, that "the scientific pursuit of knowledge alienates us from the past"; and in refusing to write "history for the sake of the living, unwittingly they may have been killing the past." See Katerberg's "History, Hope, and the Redemption of Time" 56.

8 Paul Connerton, *How Societies Remember* (Cambridge: Cambridge University Press, 1989): 14.

9 Milan Kundera, *The Book of Laughter and Forgetting* (New York: Penguin, 1986): 159.

10 Paul de Man writes that modernity consists of "a desire to wipe out whatever came earlier...[a] deliberate forgetting..." quoted in Connerton 61.

11 Katerberg, "History, Hope, and the Redemption of Time" 57.

12 Jeff Smith, *The Frugal Gourmet Keeps the Feast: Past, Present, and Future* (New York: William Morrow, 1995): 3.

13 Jeff Smith 80-81.

14 Cf. David F. Ford, *Self and Salvation: Being Transformed* (Cambridge, Cambridge University Press, 1999): 271.

15 Simone Weil, *Waiting for God* (New York: Harper and Row, 1973): 139.

CHAPTER 15

READING AND STORYTELLING: HOW NARRATIVE BUILDS FAITH

1 Daniel Taylor devotes two chapters to difficult or toxic narratives. See *The Healing Power of Stories* (New York: Doubleday, 1996): 113-154. Wayne Booth writes: "We live more or less *in* stories." All "must in fact conduct their daily business largely in stories." *The Company We Keep* (Berkeley: University of California Press, 1988): 14-15.

2 Paul Connerton, *How Societies Remember* (Cambridge: Cambridge University Press, 1989): 46.

3 Stanley Hauerwas, among others, has emphasized the narrative nature of religious experience. Narrative, he writes, is *"the form of God's salvation"* (emphasis his). We must give attention, he says, to "the narrative character of God's activity." *The Peaceable Kingdom: A Primer in Christian Ethics* (Notre Dame: University of Notre Dame Press, 1983): 29.

4 R. C. Sproul calls this approach "existential." "What I am calling for is a kind of empathy by which we try to 'crawl into the skin' of the characters we are reading about." *Knowing Scripture*

(Downers Grove, IL: InterVarsity, 1978): 66. It is important to affirm that this method of reading scripture is not a replacement of other, allegedly more "rational" methods of reading, such as the historical-critical method developed in modern Biblical studies. Intellect and reason can carry us far, but not all the way into the presence of God. It is perfectly rational to concede the limits of reason when seeking the presence of God.

5 Thelma Hall defines *lectio divina* as "a holistic way of prayer which disposes, opens and 'informs' us for the gift of contemplation God waits to give, by leading us to a meeting place with him in our deepest center....[It is] a simple and effortless way of praying via sacred scripture...." See Thelma Hall, *Too Deep for Words: Rediscovering Lectio Divina* (New York: Paulist, 1988): 7, 10.

6 Thomas Merton, *Thoughts in Solitude* (New York: Farrar, Straus and Cudahy, 1958): 48.

7 Louis Martz, ed., *George Herbert and Henry Vaughan* (Oxford: Oxford University Press, 1986): 44.

8 Wolfgang Iser, "The Reading Process: A Phenomenological Approach," *The Critical Tradition*, ed. David H. Richter, 2nd ed. (Boston: Bedford, 1998): 961.

9 George Steiner, *Real Presences* (Chicago: University of Chicago Press, 1989): 190-191.

10 A number of excellent books on the spiritual and moral power of books include Daniel Taylor, *The Healing Power of Story* (New York: Doubleday, 1996); Wayne Booth, *The Company We Keep: An Ethics of Fiction* (Berkeley: University of California Press, 1988); Robert Coles, *The Power of Stories: Teaching and the Moral Imagination* (Boston: Houghton Mifflin, 1989); and Madeleine L'Engle, *Story as Truth: The Rock that Is Higher* (Wheaton, IL: Harold Shaw, 1993). An anthology of spiritually focused readings is Darryl Tippens, Jeanne Murray Walker, and Stephen Weathers eds., *Shadow and Light: Literature and the Life of Faith*, 2nd ed. (Abilene, TX: Abilene Christian University Press, 2005).

11 Augustine, *Confessions*, trans. Henry Chadwick (Oxford: Oxford University Press, 1992): 39-40 (III.iv).

12 Simone Weil, *Waiting for God* (New York: Harper and Row, 1973): 68-69.

13 Not her real name.

14 John Milton, from "Areopagitica" in *John Milton: Complete Poems and Major Prose*, ed. Merritt Y. Hughes (Indianapolis: Odyssey, 1957): 720.

15 George Steiner 191.

16 Hauerwas: "We are unable to stand outside our histories in midair, as it were; we are destined to discover ourselves only within God's history, for God is our beginning and our end." *The Peaceable Kingdom* 29.

17 Frederick Buechner, *Telling Secrets* (New York: HarperSanFrancisco, 1991): 32.

CHAPTER 16

SUFFERING: THE FIRE THAT PURIFIES

1 Macrina Wiederkehr, *Seasons of Your Heart: Prayers & Reflections*, revised ed. (San Francisco: Harper, 1991): 17-18.

2 The question is a reoccurring theme in Elie Wiesel, *The Trial of God*, trans. Marion Wiesel (New York: Schocken, 1995).

3 *Hester panim*—the hiding of God's face—is a familiar phrase in the Old Testament. See Barbara Brown Taylor, *When God Is Silent* (Cambridge, MA: Cowley, 1998): 52.

4 For a book which suggests thoughtful, pastoral words in times of crisis, see Virgil M. Fry, *Disrupted: Finding God in Illness and Loss* (Nashville: 21st Century Christian, 1999).

5 Flannery O'Connor, *The Habit of Being: Letters of Flannery O'Connor*, ed. Sally Fitzgerald (New York: Farrar Straus Giroux, 1988): 353-354.

6 Thomas Merton, *True Solitude: Selections from the Writings of Thomas Merton* (Kansas City: Hallmark, 1969): 29-30.

7 John Donne, "Satire III"; Flannery O'Connor, *The Habit of Being: Letters of Flannery O'Connor*, ed. Sally Fitzgerald (New York: Farrar Straus Giroux, 1979); Tennyson, *In Memoriam*, Canto 96.

8 Augustine, *Confessions*, trans. Henry Chadwick (Oxford: Oxford University Press, 1991): 81 (V.viii).

9 Augustine, *Confessions* 51 (III.xii).

10 Abraham Heschel, *A Passion for Truth* (New York: Farrar Straus & Giroux, 1973): 265, 269.

11 Recently, some public figures, ministers, and clerics have routinely explained great tragedies as God's specific punishment for human sinfulness. If an earthquake devastates Pakistan or Kashmir, then someone must have done great evil. If Hurricane Katrina destroys lives and property on a massive scale, then God must be angry at the victims or the country in general. If a nation's leader falls ill, then he must have espoused the wrong political philosophy. Jesus challenges such naïve arguments.

12 Anne Lamott, *Traveling Mercies: Some Thoughts on Faith* (New York: Pantheon, 1999): 42-43.

13 Kathleen Norris, "Why the Psalms Scare Us," *Christianity Today* 15 Jul. 1996: 23.

14 Harold Kushner, *When Bad Things Happen to Good People* (New York: Avon, 1981): 120.

15 Kenneth A. Barnes, *Foot-prints to a Grave* (n.p.: self-published chapbook, 1984).

16 Kenneth Avery Barnes, *A Rough Shaking* (Meeker, OK: Seeing-Eye Press, 1988).

17 Lady Julian, *Revelations of Divine Love*, trans. Clifton Wolters (Hammondsworth, Eng.: Penguin, 1982): 103.

18 Emily Dickinson, "I Shall Know Why—when Time is over—," *The Complete Poems of Emily Dickinson*, ed. Thomas H. Johnson (Boston: Little Brown and Co., 1960): 91.

19 T. S. Eliot, *Murder in the Cathedral* (San Diego: Harcourt, Brace, Jovanovich, 1963): 70.

CHAPTER 17

SEEKING: THE END OF THE JOURNEY

1 Blaise Pascal, *Selections from the Thoughts*, ed. and trans. Arthur H. Beattie (Arlington Heights, IL: AHM, 1965): 70. Thought # 199.

2 Pascal 70, 77. Thought # 194.

3 G. K. Chesterton, *Orthodoxy: The Romance of Faith* (New York: Doubleday, 1990): 136.

4 Bruce J. Malina, *The New Testament World: Insights from Cultural Anthropology*, 3rd ed. (Louisville: Westminster John Knox, 2001): 68.

5 Malina 68-75.

6 Malina 69, 71.

7 Robert S. Root-Bernstein and Michèle Root-Bernstein, "Learning to Think with Emotion," *Chronicle of Higher Education* 14 Jan. 2000: A64; Robert S. Root-Bernstein and Michèle Root-Bernstein, *Sparks of Genius: The Thirteen Thinking Tools of the World's Most Creative People*

(Boston: Houghton Mifflin, 1999).

8 Rowan Williams, *The Wound of Knowledge* (Cambridge, MA: Cowley, 1990): 83.

9 Daniel Taylor, *In Search of Sacred Places: Looking for Wisdom on Celtic Holy Islands* (St. Paul: Bog Walk Press, 2005): 51-52.

10 Flannery O'Connor, *The Habit of Being: Letters of Flannery O'Connor*, ed. Sally Fitzgerald (New York: Farrar Straus Giroux, 1988): 354.

11 Thomas Merton, *Thoughts in Solitude* (New York: Farrar, Straus, and Cudahy, 1958): 83.

12 David J. Wolpe, *The Healer of Shattered Hearts* (New York: Penguin, 1990): 45.

13 Josef Pieper, *Faith, Hope, Love* (San Francisco: Ignatius, 1997): 167.

14 "The Wreck of the *Deutschland*," *Gerard Manley Hopkins*, ed. Catherine Phillips (Oxford: Oxford University Press, 1986): 111.

15 Dennis McLellan, "Bob Keeshan, 76, Entertained Millions as TV's Captain Kangaroo," *Los Angeles Times* 24 Jan. 2004: B22.

16 John H. Westerhoff and John D. Eusden, *The Spiritual Life: Learning East and West* (New York: Seabury, 1982): 75-76.

17 Julian of Norwich, *The Essence of Julian* (Kelowna, B.C.: Northstone Publishing, 2002): 121-122.